43-44

45-46

48 Teach me when to reveal
+ when to conceal!

#89

54
57 - cool story

#60

#69

77

84

87

91

The
Christian
Life
A HUMAN
IMPOSSIBILITY

KERRY L. SKINNER

2 Chronicles 7:14

97 - JAY

THE CHRISTIAN LIFE: A HUMAN IMPOSSIBILITY
Kerry L. Skinner

The Christian Life: A Human Impossibility
Copyright © 2012 by Kerry L. Skinner
Kerry L. Skinner-*Think LifeChange*, The Woodlands, TX 77389
www.kerryskinner.com

Library of Congress Cataloging-in-Publication Data

Skinner, Kerry L., 1955–
    The Christian Life: A Human Impossibility/Kerry L. Skinner, 1st edition
    p. cm.
    Includes bibliographic references.

    ISBN 13– 978-1-931080-05-7
    ISBN– 1-931080-05-4

1. Personal Growth–Religious aspects–Christianity
2. Counseling–Biblical teaching

Unless otherwise indicated, all Scripture quotations are taken from *The Holy Bible, New King James Version.* © 1982 by Thomas Nelson, Inc. Used by permission of Thomas Nelson, Inc.

Verses marked Phillips are taken from *J. B. Phillips: The New Testament in Modern English*, rev. ed., © J. B. Phillips 1958, 1960, 1972. Used by permission of Macmillan Publishing Company.

"Scripture quotations taken from the Amplified® Bible, Copyright © 1954, 1958, 1962, 1964, 1965, 1987 by The Lockman Foundation. Used by permission." (www.Lockman.org)

Contents

ABOUT THE AUTHOR

Kerry L. Skinner, has served in pastoral roles for more than thirty-five years with an emphasis in Christian discipleship and pastoral counseling. Through his writing and teaching, Dr. Skinner is recognized as a spokesman for biblical sufficiency. He has traveled extensively through North America teaching conferences for pastors, counselors, and lay leaders on topics such as revival, repentance, holiness, and biblical counseling.

Dr. Skinner's key mentor was Dr. Henry Brandt–a pioneer of Biblical Counseling. For over five decades, Henry Brandt–international consultant, educator, counselor, author, and conference speaker. The legacy of his ministry is written in the hearts and lives of generations of men, women, and children around the world. Dr. Skinner also served as associate to Dr. Henry Blackaby in the office of Prayer, Revival, and Spiritual Awakening for the North American Mission Board.

He has served churches in Kentucky, Texas, Florida, and Alabama. His most recent assignments were as Teaching Pastor of First Baptist Church of West Palm Beach, and Senior Associate Pastor of Cottage Hill Baptist of Mobile, Alabama.

Dr. Skinner currently serves as the Senior Pastor of Northway Church of The Woodlands, Texas. He guides a biblical counseling center using lay leadership, called the *Laity Care Center*. He and his wife, Elaine, have one son, Jason and three grandchildren.

Bachelor of Arts Degree(Christian Education), Campbellsville University
Master of Arts Degree, Southwestern Baptist Theological Seminary
Doctor of Ministry, Gordon Conwell Theological Seminary

BOOKS
Authored:
The Joy of Repentance workbook version (KLS LifeChange Ministries, 2011)
The Joy of Repentance, (KLS LifeChange Ministries, 2007)
Co-authored
Chosen to be God's Prophet with Henry Blackaby, (Thomas Nelson Publishers, 2003)
Called & Accountable with Henry Blackaby, (New Hope Publishers, 2002)
I Want to Enjoy My Children with Henry Brandt. (Multnomah Publishers, 2002)
Created to be God's Friend (workbook), with Henry Blackaby, (Thomas Nelson, 2000)
Marriage God's Way, with Henry Brandt, (Broadman/Holman, 1999)
The Power of the Call, with Henry T. Blackaby and Henry Brandt, (Broadman/Holman, 1997)
The Heart of the Problem (book and workbook), with Henry Brandt, (Broadman/Holman, 1995)
The Word for the Wise with Henry Brandt, Broadman/Holman, 1995)
Breaking Free from the Bondage of Sin with Henry Brandt, (Harvest House Publishers, 1994)

www.kerryskinner.com

DEDICATION

Since my early days of ministry, God has invested in my life through countless individuals. From childhood to volunteer ministry beginnings and from college experiences to pastoral positions, God has placed incredible people in my life at the right time and place to guide me in learning what it means to be a dedicated disciple of Jesus Christ.

To my mom and dad who established me in the Christian faith, teaching me to remain faithful to Jesus Christ.

To my first pastor I served with in my first full-time ministry position, Ken Hensarling, and his wonderful wife Rosa, who are friends to this day. I am indeed grateful for the investment they made in me as a young and inexperienced minister. They helped shape my life for God's glory.

To Avery Willis, Jr., now gone to be with The Lord, helped me know the beginnings of what it meant to, "Deny self and take up the cross of Christ." I am continuing to learn that lesson which began in the experience of a 1980 MasterLife workshop.

To Henry Brandt, also gone to be with The Lord, sharpened my skills tremendously in the area of biblical counseling. I miss those times we shared together in writing, leading conferences, and as we visited together in our respective homes.

To Henry Blackaby who gave me incredible opportunities across North America to share the message of repentance. He is a man of God who helped me stay God focused in ministry.

To Keith Thomas, also gone to be with The Lord, who allowed me the opportunities to develop biblical counseling centers as well as opportunities to partner with him in ministry.

To Rodney Mills who is a present partner in ministry. He spurs me on to creativity and focus as we seek to make dedicated disciples of Jesus Christ.

Most of all, to Elaine, my wife of 40 years. She is my prayer partner, friend, and the love of my life. She has always been the encourager who helps me to press on with the work God has set before us as a team.

INTRODUCTION

Learning the basics of Christianity is relatively simple–if knowledge of the how to's are all that interest you. Simply listing the commands of Christ does not require a massive amount of time nor an in depth study. Putting into practice the commands of Christ is quite different! To do what Christ instructs requires study, devotion, prayer, and daily experience.

I suppose for years I worked on Christianity the same way many others went about the task. Making sure I spent time with daily Bible reading and prayer time was the main focus. Other than that, I attempted to **not** do all the evil things that Christians were to avoid. I reasoned that if I avoided the evil activities, then I would be a good Christian. But, I had missed out on the most important part of Christianity–learning to walk in the Spirit! Life in Christ is an incredibly fulfilling way to live. Why would anyone want to live the Christian life with mere human effort?

God used positive and negative experiences, as well as particular circumstances, to lead me in beginning the discovery of what it meant to walk in the Spirit. Through the years I discovered that human ability falls short in teaching you to walk in the Spirit. The fruit of the Spirit has nothing to do with other people or human experiences–rather it is a by product of a relationship with God.

If that is true, then the Christian life is a human impossibility. I pray as you read this book, you will develop further in your relationship with God, helping you to know, understand, and experience how the Christian life can only be learned and lived as you walk in His Spirit. As you do, you will fully understand what Jesus meant when He said,

> *I am the vine, you are the branches. He who abides in Me, and I in him, bears much fruit; for without Me you can do nothing.*
> **John 15:5 NKJV**

Kerry L. Skinner

Chapter One

Walking in the Spirit–What Does It Mean?

Many subjects in the Bible are simple to understand, while others are more complex. Consider the subject of being born again. It is simple to say that a person needs to be born again, but much more complex to explain what must happen in the human soul for a person to be born again. When a person truly repents of his/her sin, understanding comes to one's spirit about the dynamics of salvation, but it is still difficult to put in words what truly happens when repentance occurs.

Consider another subject found in the Bible–*walking in the Spirit*. When assigned the task of teaching the truth of God's Word, simplicity is necessary. Of course, making something simple is one of the most difficult things to accomplish. A person can expound on a verse or a word from the Bible and make it complex or simple. Concepts taught in the secular classroom can also be made complex or simple. When a teacher finishes a lecture, the student may have pages of notes that are not yet comprehended. Students take notes even though the words are not fully absorbed in their mind. Someone once said that a college lecture is the process of transferring the notes from the professor to the student without going through the mind of either!

If you read God's Word often, but do not apply its simple truths, you become full of knowledge. Acquired knowledge without practical application leaves one wondering how this really works out in real life.

While Jesus taught in simple terms, many times the disciples did not understand His meaning. His description of a believer used simple terms. He referred to believers as being like a *light* or like *salt*. Parables simple illustrations such as coins, buried treasure, or a to the sea, to describe deep spiritual truth.

Biblical Walking

Walking in the Spirit is a spiritual experience that few know how to explain. The term *walk* is understandable. The term *Spirit* is more difficult. In Galatians 5, Paul used these terms together. Without a doubt, this is the major place in Scripture where these terms are used together.

> *I say then:* **Walk in the Spirit**, *and you shall not fulfill the lust of the flesh. For the flesh lusts against the Spirit, and the Spirit against the flesh; and these are contrary to one another, so that you do not do the things that you wish. But if you are* **led by the Spirit**, *you are not under the law. Now the works of the flesh are evident, which are: adultery, fornication, uncleanness, lewdness...*

Galatians 5:16-19

In this short passage, Paul reveals two lists that are polar opposites. Though verse sixteen is the primary passage related to this idea of *walking in the Spirit,* it also occurs throughout the Old and New Testament.

Digging through the Scriptures revealed this discovery of words related to walking.

	# of Verses	# of Appearances in Verses
Walk	211	220
Walked	92	93
Walking	29	29
TOTAL	**332**	**342**

Such a simple phrase as, "walk in the Spirit" reveals incredible truth. Before beginning the process, I assumed that most of these occurrences would refer to someone *walking* across a field or up a mountain, or the children of Israel *walking* in the desert or possibly Noah *walking* on the ark. Reading through each passage revealed an unexpected finding.

This surprising discovery uncovered that only 87 of the 332 appearances of the different forms of the word *walk* refer to the generic sense of someone physically walking. Every other time it represents the idea of *walking in the ways of God.*

Instead of reading of Noah *walking* on the ark, the major emphasis is on statements such as, "Noah *walked* with God" (Gen. 6:9) or, "You shall *walk* in all the ways which the LORD your God has commanded you" (Deut. 5:33). This *walking* refers to a person becoming intimately acquainted with God. Noah spent t · ꞏ ˏ the heart of God. Noah prayed to God and meditate. ..am *walked* with God. This does not mean that they physically *walked* with God.

Further reading of the Old Testament reveals situations like this, "he *walked* in the way of his father who *walked* with God." Others statements show people who *did not* have an intimate *walk* with God, such as, "he *walked* in the ways of his father." 1 Samuel reveals one of these situations.

> *But his sons did not walk in his ways; they turned aside after dishonest gain, took bribes, and perverted justice.*
> **1 Samuel 8:3**

Physical Walking

What does it mean to walk physically? The dictionary describes *walk* as an active position of motion with intentionality getting from one point to another. That means that *walking* requires activity.

Paul did not say, "Stand in the Spirit" nor did he say, "Sit in the Spirit." Rather, Paul said, "*Walk* in the Spirit." *Walking* is an active motion. *Walking in the Spirit is an active movement* in the life of a believer. *Walking* in the Spirit is not static, it is active. Can you *walk* backwards? Yes, but illustrations of a person *walking* to town is not pictured as a person *walking* backwards to town. *Walking* implies a forward motion. A person is intentional and active when *walking*. Some have said that *walking* is simply controlled falling. Once you begin to *walk* you have to continue, not stop in the middle of a step, if you are going to arrive at your destination.

Walking in the Ways of God

There is an overwhelming number of Bible passages that describe the people of God *walking in the ways of God*. *Walking* in these ways signified their relationship with God. Take note of these verses:

You shall <u>walk</u> in all the ways which the LORD your God has commanded you, that you may live and that it may be well with you, and that you may prolong your days in the land which you shall possess.

Deuteronomy 5:33

You shall observe My judgments and keep My ordinances, to <u>walk</u> in them: I am the LORD your God.

Leviticus 18:4

And he blessed Joseph, and said: "God, before whom my fathers Abraham and Isaac <u>walked</u>, The God who has fed me all my life long to this day.

Genesis 48:15

Walking is relationship oriented in the Bible. To *walk* in His ways, *walk* in His commandments, *walk* in His statutes, means to do what He says. In the New Testament, Jesus says, "If you love Me, keep My commandments" (John 14:15). *Walking* in His ways shows one is in a vibrant relationship with Him.

Suppose you decide to go on a walk with someone. Why would two people agree to walk together? People walk together for safety, they have something to discuss, or they want to encourage one another to exercise. People choose a particular person to walk with because their minds are together. There is something in common with you and the other person that causes you to want to walk together. You will walk with someone if you enjoy their company. Suppose however, that in the middle of the walk you get mad at one another. How long do you think the two of you will keep walking together? Soon after this, you would be walking one direction and the other person in another direction. The Scripture states,

Can two walk together, unless they are agreed?

Amos 3:3

The answer is no! If you are going to *walk* in the Lord's ways, you must agree with His ways. The moment you disagree with God, you will stop *walking in the Spirit*! That is exactly what happened with Adam and Eve when they disagreed with God.

And they heard the sound of the LORD God walking in the garden in the cool of the day, and Adam and his wife hid themselves from the presence of the LORD God among the trees of the garden.
Genesis 3:8

God was not physically *walking* in the garden. This Scripture symbolizes the fact that His presence overwhelmed Adam and Eve in the garden. God's relationship is described using the term *walk*. Adam and Eve hid themselves because they had broken His ways, commandments, and laws.

If you do not agree with Him, you will not *walk* with Him. If you do not *walk* with Him, there will be consequences. The Scripture reveals,

"Then, if you walk contrary to Me, and are not willing to obey Me, I will bring on you seven times more plagues, according to your sins."
Leviticus 26:21

In the Old and New Testament, God filled His people with His Spirit for particular assignments.

And I have filled him with the Spirit of God, in wisdom, in understanding, in knowledge, and in all manner of workmanship.
Exodus 31:3

You who are named the house of Jacob: "Is the Spirit of the LORD restricted? Are these His doings? Do not My words do good To him who walks uprightly?
Micah 2:7

Through the prophet Micah, God was not suggesting that a person have straight posture as you *walk*. Rather, this passage illustrates that your heart, mind, and soul must *walk* in agreement with God in order to be used of God. *Walking* with God in this way requires one to be *filled* with His Spirit.

The Indwelling and The Filling of the Spirit

There is a difference between the *indwelling* Spirit and the *filling* of the Spirit. In Romans, Paul writes to a group of believers who have the Holy Spirit living in them. He says,

[1] There is therefore now no condemnation to those who are in

Christ Jesus, who do not <u>walk</u> according to the flesh, but according to the Spirit.

⁴ ...that the righteous requirement of the law might be fulfilled in us who do not <u>walk</u> according to the flesh but according to the Spirit.

Romans 8:1, 4

But you are not living the life of the flesh, you are living the life of the Spirit, if the [Holy] Spirit of God [really] dwells within you [directs and controls you]. But if anyone does not possess the [Holy] Spirit of Christ, he is none of His [he does not belong to Christ, is not truly a child of God].

Romans 8:9, AMP

Did you know that if you have been born again, the Holy Spirit has taken up residence within you? How often is the Holy Spirit living within you? All the time! The Holy Spirit never departs from you–He dwells in you. When you were born again, Jesus said that He would give you His Spirit who would guide you in all things (John 14:26).

My last name is Skinner. I was born into the Skinner family. I will always be a Skinner. I have Skinner blood in my veins. If my dad ever said that he disowned me, I would still be a Skinner. Why? Because I am a Skinner by birth. A broken fellowship with my dad does not change my relationship, but it does change how I relate to him.

If you are a born again believer in Christ, you have a new relationship. When Christ came into your life He put within you His Holy Spirit. You are filled with His Holy Spirit.

What Does Indwelling Mean?

1. This indwelling occurs when we first believe. It does not occur twenty years later but rather when you are born again. (Rom. 5:5, 2 Tim. 2:4)
2. The indwelling of the Holy Spirit occurs one time. It is once for all. When Jesus Christ comes into your life as your Lord and Savior, His Spirit takes up permanent residence in you.
3. The indwelling of the Holy Spirit is for all believers. Simply claiming to be a Christian does not necessarily mean you are a Christian (Matt. 7:21).

What makes a person different is not that you claim that Jesus is Lord, not that you believe facts such as, He was born of a virgin, or that He lived a sinless life. Believing the facts does not make you born again.

> *You believe that there is one God. You do well. Even the demons believe–and tremble!*
> **James 2:19**

The demons believe the facts about Jesus but they are not born again and will not be in heaven. A born-again believer has the indwelling of the Holy Spirit at the moment they believe, a blessing that no evil spirit can experience.

Believers *are not commanded* to be indwelt or possessed by the Holy Spirit, born-again people *are* possessed by the Holy Spirit. The indwelling does not indicate direction in life but position in life.

> *Or do you not know that your body is the temple of the Holy Spirit who is in you, whom you have from God, and you are not your own? For you were bought at a price; therefore glorify God in your body and in your spirit, which are God's.*
> **1 Corinthians 6:19-20**

> *[37] On the last day, that great day of the feast, Jesus stood and cried out, saying, "If anyone thirsts, let him come to Me and drink. [38] He who believes in Me, as the Scripture has said, out of his heart will flow rivers of living water." [39] But this He spoke concerning the Spirit, whom those believing in Him would receive; for the Holy Spirit was not yet given, because Jesus was not yet glorified.*
> **John 7:37-39**

> *[13] In Him you also trusted, after you heard the word of truth, the gospel of your salvation; in whom also, having believed, you were sealed with the Holy Spirit of promise, [14] who is the guarantee of our inheritance until the redemption of the purchased possession, to the praise of His glory.*
> **Ephesians 1:13-14**

When God put His Holy Spirit of promise in you, He put Him there until the redemption of the purchased possession. That means a born again person is permanently indwelt!

What Does Being Filled Mean?

Paul addresses a different issue in Galatians 5:16. Paul states, "walk in the Spirit and you will not fulfill the desires of the flesh." This *walking in the Spirit* is an active relationship with God.

So what is different about being *indwelt* and being *filled* by the Spirit?

1. Being filled is a repeated experience. Being filled by God's Spirit is something you must continually ask God to do.
2. Being filled can be for specific times and assignments. (Acts 4:8)
3. Being filled is for all believers but only affects those who are yielded to God.
4. Being filled can in effect be lost when believers are rebelling against the will of God in their lives.
5. Being filled can be renewed through repentance.
6. Being filled results in the power of the Spirit at work in your life.

Being filled by the Spirit is best understood as being the opposite of being filled by the flesh. Paul reveals this difference when he said to, "walk in the Spirit so you do not fulfill the desires of the flesh."

Legalism

Many people grow up with legalism as their foundation of the Christian life. Legalistic teaching sounds more like this, "Don't do this and don't do that, and you will be a good Christian." This kind of teaching seldom focuses on what it means to *walk* in the Spirit but rather focuses on what not to do! Learning how *not to walk in the flesh* does not necessarily mean you ever learned *to walk in the Spirit*. Unbelievers can live a good moral lifestyle but that does not mean they are walking in the Spirit. Powerful kingdom living cannot be accomplished unless you are born again.

Illustration

How do you describe being filled with the Spirit? Imagine a bottle of water representing you as a person. The bottle represents your physical body and the water represents the Spirit of God living in you. Suppose the bottle is not completely full of water. If you remove the cap from the bottle and begin to pour more water into the bottle, the bottle is *being filled* with water.

The bottle already contains the Holy Spirit. This filling with more water does not represent the indwelling of the Holy Spirit but the filling of the Holy Spirit. The key is not what you are being filled with but it is the means by which you are filled. For example, the bottle can do nothing of itself (John 15:5). We can do nothing without Christ. To fill the bottle with the water just to say it has water in it is not the focus. An *outside source* has to fill the bottle. The bottle cannot fill itself.

The water is not the act of *walking* in the Spirit. The water is the indwelling Spirit. The bottle contains the Spirit and has the capacity to act upon what is inside. Ephesians 5:18 clarifies this fact.

> *And do not be drunk with wine, in which is dissipation; but be filled with the Spirit,*
> **Ephesians 5:18**

Suppose you observe a person *walking* down the street in a disorderly fashion. In fact, it is obvious he is drunk. Then you notice that the person is someone you know who claims to be Christian. Upon further observation, you notice another person *walking* beside him and it is obvious the second person is not drunk. Which one is the most godly? Most would not think it is the first person who is drunk. But, what if the second person who is *walking* straight, claimed to be a Christian, yet he was not *walking* in the Spirit. Which is worse? To not *walk* in the Spirit, is a Holy offense against God.

God indwells you by His Spirit to guide you in His ways. Throughout the Old Testament, God wanted His people to live according to His ways, statutes, judgments, and His commandments. To *walk* in the Spirit you simply have to do what God says with a heart that is right toward Him.

The key to a water bottle is not that it is a bottle and that you can put water in it. A bottle could be filled with dirty water also. The vessel is not as important as the contents of the vessel. We must be filled with the Spirit to be a vessel of righteousness (Rom. 6:13).

Don't be drunk with wine but be filled with the Spirit! God wants us to do what He says and live according to the Spirit. We must come under the control of the Spirit like a drunk comes under control of the spirits. God's Spirit begins to control you to do things you would not do simply because you have human abilities. When you *walk* in the ways of God, He begins to do things in and through your life that you could never accomplish with simple human ability. In that sense, a person who knew you before you started *walking* in God's ways would think you are drunk because you look and act so different from your old ways.

What Does It Mean To Walk In The Spirit?

To *walk* is to be controlled by the Spirit of God living within you.

Think of the word–*walk.* Have you ever noticed a person walking a big dog? Who is *walking* who? Sometimes the dog leads the person where they do not intend to go. The indwelling of the Spirit is within you. As you obey and live according to the ways of the Spirit who lives within you, He takes control and takes you places where you would not have necessarily traveled. Now, it is His Spirit leading you, not your flesh.

Imagine a huge sail on a sailboat. When the wind hits the sail, the wind fills the sail. The wind takes the boat in the direction of the wind. The key to walking in the Spirit is yielding and submitting your life to Christ. To be filled is to voluntarily surrender your life to God, giving up your rights, and submitting to His ways. His Spirit will take you like wind in a sail, wherever He wills.

Remember the bottle of water illustration. Suppose the bottle is almost full of anger. What if you want to fill the bottle with the peace of God? How do you fill a bottle with peace when it is already filled with anger? You must empty out the anger before filling it with something else. God will not force you to walk in love, joy, and peace, but He has indwelt you with His Spirit to give you the potential to live that way. You cannot *walk* in His ways unless you yield to Him, surrender yourself, and give up your rights. *Walking* in the Spirit means to depend upon the Spirit–to actively choose to follow God in all His ways–not your ways!

What does that mean practically for us? Galatians 5:19-21 stat

> *Now the works of the flesh are evident, which are: adultery, for-nication, uncleanness, lewdness idolatry, sorcery, hatred, conten-tions, jealousies, outbursts of wrath, selfish ambitions, dissen-sions, heresies, envy, murders, drunkenness, revelries, and the like; of which I tell you beforehand, just as I also told you in time past, that those who practice such things will not inherit the kingdom of God.*

You cannot permanently live in these ways and have other people fooled into believing that you are indwelt by the Spirit. The key term is that the works of the flesh are *evident (obvious)*. But if, you live by the fruit of the Spirit, it will also be obvious.

You cannot live both ways at the same time. Though you can be in-dwelt by the Holy Spirit, that is, have a relationship with God through Christ that will never be broken, you can also be out of fellowship with God and be susceptible to all these sins.

King David was known as a man after God's own heart. In his youth, he was a shepherd boy. With God at the center of his heart, David ap-proached the assignment to meet the giant—Goliath. King Saul told Da-vid to put on all of the king's armor. But the armor was bigger than David! He could not *walk* in this armor. David had put on the weight of the world to try and do God's work. God empowered David to shed the armor and do something that God's Spirit would enable him to ac-complish. David was successful, because He *walked* in the ways of God.

Years later, God anointed David as king of Israel. David knew God intimately and followed Him. But, a time came when David went up to a rooftop and looked down on a young woman. He lusted after her. He committed adultery, had a child from that relationship, and had her husband murdered.

In the sense that we talk about in the New Testament, David was indwelt by the Holy Spirit—that was permanent. But, temporarily, he took back his rights, chose his ways—not God's ways—and destruction came to him. Later in the Psalms we hear his heart through writing. Da-vid repented deeply and God restored His fellowship with David. The Scripture records David saying,

Against You, You only, have I sinned, and done this evil in Your sight–that You may be found just when You speak, and blameless when You judge.

Psalm 51:4

We know that David sinned against other people. But he saw his primary sin as against God. David had a relationship with God which he broke. If David had never broken fellowship with God, he would never have contemplated adultery and murder.

The greatest sin for the believer is to *not walk according to the controlling ways of the Spirit* who lives within you. When you choose to not *walk* in His ways, you become susceptible to every wrong way. Praise God though, that by His grace, you do not have to live that way.

What is Walking In The Spirit?

Walking in the Spirit means to *walk* in the ways of God instead of your own ways and requires you to *Think LifeChange*! When you are changed by God's Spirit, your thinking, attitudes, and actions will change! People will know that you are different as they observe your lifestyle. Evidences of a changed life will be measured, observed, and considered by those around you.

But how would you know if you have been changed? Simply observe your life in the everyday practical aspects of daily living and ask yourself this question: "What evidence is there in this area of my life that shows I am *walking* in God's ways instead of my ways?"

The remaining chapters of this book will help you identify *LifeChange* and help you to *Think LifeChange* in many areas of Christian living.

Chapter Two

Are You Content?

Are you satisfied and content with life? Would your friends, family, and co-workers want to model their life after your example of satisfaction and contentment?

If you are disturbed, not at ease, tense, or frustrated with the events and people in your life, then you need contentment and satisfaction. To walk in the Spirit gives you a focus that is out of this world! When you walk in the flesh, the focus is on events, news, and relationships that may not be focused on God. The Scripture states,

> *I say then: Walk in the Spirit, and you shall not fulfill the lust of the flesh.*

Galatians 5:16

Serving my first church after graduating from college revealed my spirit. Though my dad was a pastor, and I learned a few things about ministry that not everyone experiences, it was much different observing people from the eyes of a church staff member than by simply observing people as a church member. As a recent graduate from college with a degree in Christian education, I thought I knew how to direct the operations of the church. If *those* people at *that* church would just listen to me, then surely I would be satisfied and so would they!

Serving as an associate pastor the first few months of being in the church, my wife and I became acquainted with and developed a deep respect for a godly woman in the church. You can imagine how shocked I was when she came to be and stated, "Kerry, I read my Bible every day and pray. I am very faithful in my attendance and service to the church. But, there is something missing in my life. There has to be more to the Christian life than what I am experiencing. Can you show me how to experience more in my Christian life?" That conversation was a defining moment in my life.

Knowledge that I had acquired from growing up in a pastor's home and from attending a Christian college surely would give me an answer for her. But when she asked that question, I was shocked because I thought she was more godly than me! Why would she ask me such a question? As a new pastor, I thought I could learn many things from her about how to be a better Christian. I did not have an answer for her. Over the next few months, God began to develop something in my life that has helped me to never be the same again.

I knew that walking in the Spirit was different than walking in the flesh. The real issue for me was how do you walk in the Spirit? Most believers have learned how to avoid walking in the flesh but have not learned how to walk in the Spirit. Many have learned how not to do certain wrong things and stay away from fleshly desires but have never really learned how to walk in the Spirit. They know there is more to the Christian life than what they are experiencing and they really desire it, but how do they achieve that experience?

The apostle Paul describes the fruit of this walking in the Spirit. "But the fruit of the Spirit is love, joy, peace, longsuffering, kindness, goodness, faithfulness..." (Gal. 5:22). How would you know if this fruit is being experienced? One way you would know is that you would have a deep satisfaction and contentment in life.

When we watch the news and hear of events such as the tsunami that devastated southeast Asia, we discover that some of our problems are not as big a problem as we thought. When we observe life threatening situations of others, our perspective changes. "And having food and clothing, with these we shall be content" (1 Tim. 6:8). But is this really enough for us? Are we content with just these few things in life? How would you know the difference between the satisfaction that Christ brings as opposed to what the world can bring?

Mark Twain once played a trick on his friends that revealed a little dissatisfaction. He said, "I once sent a dozen of my friends a telegram saying, 'Flee at once, all is discovered! They all left town immediately.'"

Jeff Foxworthy seemed to be content with his style of life when he said, "I have never been jealous, not even when my dad finished fifth grade a year before I did."

Benjamin Franklin stated, "Contentment makes poor men rich. Discontentment makes rich men poor." A wrong attitude such as discontentment is easily acquired and can quickly blow truth out of proportion. The resulting state of mind evidences one is not walking in the Spirit. If we observe ourselves for a week, we will discover whether we are walking in the flesh or the Spirit. Someone once said that contentment is the attitude of accepting whatever God supplies and being happy with it. That is so true! The great preacher, Charles Spurgeon once said, "Remember that a man's contentment is in his mind, not in the extent of his possessions."

The contented person can never be ruined. The satisfied person in Christ, who walks in the Spirit, will not be ruined because the satisfaction comes not from what is going on around them, or from the people whom they associate, but in a relationship with Jesus Christ.

Once, after leading a conference with Dr. Henry Brandt, we were having dinner with a pastor. Dr. Brandt was sitting at the table eating his soup–slowly. The pastor began telling Dr. Brandt everything that was going wrong in his life and in his church. He stated repeatedly how much of a struggle he was experiencing. Dr. Brandt continued eating his soup while this miserable pastor was expressing his discontent. Finally, the frustrated pastor said, "Dr. Brandt, don't you have some advice for me?" Dr. Brandt stopped eating his soup for a moment, spoon still in hand, and said, "Get happy!" and went back to eating his soup. It was a humorous moment to me but impacting for the pastor. Contentment is thanking God for what you currently have and being happy to live with what you do have.

sment

ontent with your current position at work, home, or

2. Have you noticed it does not take long for uncooperative people to reveal your heart?
3. Have you noticed that children can quickly reveal your heart?
4. Are you satisfied with how you are serving the Lord?
5. Are you satisfied with what is going on in the life of your church?

One experience of worship is not enough to keep you going. You must have a continual filling of fruit. If you set a bowl of fruit on a table for a few days, the fruit will become rotten. Spiritual fruit is the same. Yesterday's victory is not enough to carry you through today. You must walk in the Spirit consistently, moment by moment, and day after day.

It is amazing how often people approach others for help concerning issues they believe are unique problems. They believe their problem has never occurred in the history of the world. But, as they reveal their story, those listening realize that the story has happened numerous times in many situations. A good listener recognizes there is something they are missing. They are not walking in the Spirit, they must be walking in the flesh. The answer to their problem is to become satisfied with the place where they find themselves. Being happy and rejoicing and praising God for what He is doing in and through their life is the missing element. Instead of focusing on all the little details that bring discouragement to them, they must refocus and *Think LifeChange.*

Watching the news should wake us up enough to realize that the world is facing death and destruction. Yet, a negative outcome in our world is not the end of the story. Christ lives in us and gives us hope. While many in the world are simply trying to survive their physical needs, others have everything they need but are not content with what they possess. There is a missing element. Could it be that we are thirsting for more instead of enjoying what we possess?

Greed is the opposite of contentment. Greed makes a person continually thirst for more and yet never be satisfied. It is like drinking salt water. Even though salt water is not good for you, when you drink it, you thirst for more. If you continue to drink the salt water, death is the outcome.

What is the one thing you believe you need in your life to be content? Maybe it is a better position at work, how you are honored at church, a different relationship, or a change in your home life. Of course the real answer is Jesus Christ. But, what difference do you see Christ making in the midst of your crisis. Is He making a difference that gives you the ability to continue in God's Word daily? To be consistent in your prayer life? To be faithful in giving your time, talents, and treasures? If you are not seeing Christ's magnificent work in your life, you are disoriented to walking in His ways.

Unhappiness can drive you to wrong thinking. It might sound like this, "God, will you give me a better position at work since I hate my current position!" It is amazing how people think they will be content if they can just let others know how discontent they feel. If they can show others how discontented they are, then perhaps those people will give them what they want so they can be satisfied. Have you noticed that unhappy people clearly communicate to friends that they are unhappy? Their lifestyle certainly does not demonstrate how to walk in the Spirit. They may even believe that if they walk in the flesh long enough, that it will win the day and change situations and people.

Philippians chapter 4 gives stimulating thoughts from the Apostle Paul.

> *Not that I speak in regard to need, for I have learned in whatever state I am, to be content.*

Philippians 4:11

Whether you live in Texas, Florida, or Ohio, your geographical position does not determine the condition of your spiritual life. If you cannot be content where you are today, you will never enjoy tomorrow, no matter where you live. Contentment is not directly related to where you are or who is around you. Paul had been shipwrecked, beaten, stoned, and thrown in prison. Yet, he wrote many letters from prison to encourage us. He came to the place where he could be content and satisfied wherever he was as long as he was walking in the Spirit. The circumstances around him did not change his heart, walking in the Spirit brought a change in him. He further stated,

> *I know how to be abased, and I know how to abound. Everywhere and in all things I have learned both to be full and to be hungry, both to abound and to suffer need.*
>
> **Philippians 4:12-13**

True satisfaction is a lifelong learning process. You can act content when you are not content. Satisfaction becomes reality as you learn to walk in the Spirit in such a way that contentment becomes your life-style. Convincing everyone in your life that you are satisfied when you really are not satisfied results in dismay and resentment. There is nothing more empty and dissatisfying in the life of a believer than to act content in front of people who seem to be content.

Have you noticed?

- There are two kinds of people in this world. Those who are content and those who are trying to be content.
- Those who are walking in peace and those who are attempting to walk in peace.
- Those who are walking in joy and those who are attempting to walk in joy.

When you attempt to be content and satisfied in life by the power of your own flesh, it will be obvious to you that you are not content. Remember,

> *Walk in the Spirit, and you shall not fulfill the lust of the flesh.*
>
> **Galatians 5:16**

Everyone faces unpleasant events. Think of a recent event in your life that was unpleasant, maybe even demoralizing. Did you simply endured that event? Perhaps you complained about how you were mistreated and you never grew to be content with what happened. Contentment is not strengthened by complaining about your current situation. Usually God releases you to a new assignment only when you are satisfied with your current assignment. Complaining about your current job, telling everyone how miserable you are and how much you dislike the position, does not cause others to give you a promotion.

I remember serving as a pastor at a church, but I wanted to leav. that church and start a new beginning–anywhere else. The problem was not the church, the people, or the staff, it was my own heart. I was not content with the situation in which I found myself. I was in a miserable situation. Satisfaction had departed from my heart and mind. I simply was focusing on my own flesh. I would pray to God, "Would you let me go to a better church?" I thought that if I told God how I hated my life that He would give me a better life. His answer: silence!

Tell God how miserable you are and God will bless you with something new and fresh, right? What I discovered was that God releases you to a new assignment only when you become *satisfied* with your current assignment. That does not mean that when you do become satisfied that He will give you a new assignment. But, you will be thoroughly equipped by Him and ready for any new assignment He wants to give to you. If you are miserable in your work and you resign your position, you will take yourself with you to the new assignment! God is not wanting to hinder us, He is wanting to release us with new assignments–but He is waiting for a heart that can walk in contentment and satisfaction. As you walk with God, you will see character development in your life. Can you imagine the Apostle Paul saying, "Lord, I was shipwrecked. I'm not going anywhere until you bring a yacht to take me to the next location. I am going to complain and complain until You bring that beautiful boat by here!" Please understand, you cannot complain to God and convince Him to bless you when your character does not match the assignment He wants to give you. As God builds character in your life through walking in the Spirit, He will lead you to the next step.

> *Let your conduct be without covetousness; be content with such things as you have. For He Himself has said, "I will never leave you nor forsake you.*

Hebrews 13:5

That is great news! God will never leave you nor forsake you. That brings great comfort and also great conviction. Comfort when going through difficult times, conviction when you are behind closed doors and no one else can see what you are doing, *He is there*–He will never leave you. God knows what is going on in your thought life.

If God never leaves nor forsakes you, then His Holy Spirit will bring conviction when you stray from Him. Why is it so important that you return to Him? Because you will not fully understand God's practical manifest presence in your life while walking in the flesh. It will seem as though God is absent when your life does not match up with the Spirit of Christ living in you. When that happens, there must be a change in life. You must turn back to God so you can experience the manifest presence of God.

Paul helped us understand this lifestyle when he wrote,

> *For to me, to live is Christ, and to die is gain.*
> **Philippians 1:21**

That means we are to be content with life. We are to be content in facing death. To walk in the Spirit allows you to face whatever comes your way. This may sound easy, but all of us have failed to walk in the Spirit from time to time. When troubles come, we may fail to experience the peace that only Christ can bring. God allows us to be in the middle of a crisis whether or not we are prepared. Who knows when the next crisis is coming? No one. Then how critical is it that we stay up to date with God? It is absolutely imperative that we continue to walk in the Spirit moment by moment.

Guiding Questions and Thoughts for Contentment

1. Are you happy with what God has provided?
2. Contentment is the attitude of accepting whatever God provides and being happy with it.
3. Contentment is living for others. "Let nothing be done through selfish ambition or conceit, but in lowliness of mind let each esteem others better than himself" (Phil. 2:3).
4. Contentment is not dependent on circumstances. "Not that I speak in regard to need, for I have learned in whatever state I am, to be content: I know how to be abased, and I know how to abound. Everywhere and in all things I have learned both to be full and to be hungry, both to abound and to suffer need" (Phil. 4:11-12).

5. Contentment is spending time in praise. "Rejoice in the Lord always. Again I will say, rejoice!" (Phil. 4:4).
6. Contentment is spending time in prayer. "Be anxious for nothing, but in everything by prayer and supplication, with thanksgiving, let your requests be made known to God; and the peace of God, which surpasses all understanding, will guard your hearts and minds through Christ Jesus" (Phil. 4:6-7).
7. Contentment is spending time with positive models. "Brethren, join in following my example, and note those who so walk, as you have us for a pattern" (Phil. 3:17).
8. Do others observe the work of Christ in your life?

Life is enhanced as you spend time with godly people. Make sure you spend time with the right people and listen to the right things. Make sure you do not get drawn off course by spending time with negative and cynical personalities.

If God has shown you a troublesome part of your life, be careful what you do next! Avoid the attempt to solve your own problem by thinking, "Now that I know what the problem is, I will fix it. I will be better this week." Walking in the Spirit has nothing to do with your ability to act better. Walking in the Spirit is humanly impossible. In fact, it is totally out of this world!

God is not waiting for us to make a new commitment. God is waiting for us to say, "God, I surrender my ways to Your ways. Please give me the power of Your Spirit to be lived out through my life. God let Your Spirit flow through me so that those around me notice that what is coming out of my life has nothing to do with my flesh but is evidence of walking in Your Spirit."

Remember, walking in the Spirit has nothing to do with other people. The fruit of the Spirit is between you and God.

Chapter Three

I Would'nt Say That If I Were You

"I wouldn't say that if I were you." Have you ever been visiting with people at a social event and you just blurted something out of your mouth that surprised you? You wondered, "Where did that come from? I didn't mean to say that!" You may have been thinking about what you said, but you did not mean for it to be heard in public! On other occasions a friend may have shared with you how upset he/she was with someone and they were about to say something you think they would later regret. Your goal is to redirect them so they do not say something they will have trouble recovering from later. Opportunities to say things that we really should not say occur frequently.

Roger Williams, a Protestant theologian who began the Providence Colony in 1636, said, "I'm a Puritan at heart. I believe like the Puritans except I am a separatist and I believe what the Puritans believe but I live by what I believe not the way they live." He further said, "I am one who practices what I preach." Of course, the state of Massachusetts, and all the leaders, removed him from the state because he objected to their practices. Many times Roger Williams was right, but he didn't have godly discretion in saying the right thing, the right way, at the right time.

Many Christians have the idea that the way to walk in the Spirit is determined by their own personal knowledge and abilities. But, walking in the Spirit has nothing to do with human abilities and ideas, but rather, is best explained by complete surrender to God and His Ways.

A surrendered heart leads us to godly discretion.

The discretion of a man makes him slow to anger, and his glory is to overlook a transgression.

Proverbs 19:11

The dictionary defines discretion from four major aspects.

1. The trait of judging wisely and objectively.
2. The power of making free choices unconstrained by external agencies.
3. Knowing how to avoid embarrassment or distress.
4. Refined taste or tact.

Public speakers know that they are under pressure to give a good presentation. There are times when presenters of a speech, a sermon, or a lesson fall short of their goal–the result–a poor speech. If this happens, commenting on the speech needs discretion.

Maybe you have heard some of the tactless, yet humorous responses to a bad speech. Godly discretion would not use these examples:

1. "Never better."
2. "Were you ever good?"
3. "Wow, you should have been in the audience!"
4. "You've got talent you haven't even used!"
5. "Nobody does that kind of teaching like you do."
6. "If I hadn't heard it myself, I wouldn't have believed it."
7. "I expected the seminar to be good but you fooled me."
8. "I loved the ending."

For about ten years, I traveled around North America at the pace of about a hundred flights a year. I remember several times when airline pilots made humorous statements over the intercom. One time a pilot said "We want to thank you for giving us the business as much as we enjoy taking you for a ride." During his welcome message, another pilot said, "This airline is pleased to have some of the best flight attendants in the industry. Unfortunately none of them are on this flight." That was not the best thing to say but we got his point!

There is a good way and a right time to make statemen
are bad ways and inappropriate times to convey your thoug

A good man deals graciously and lends; he will guide his affairs
with discretion.

Psalm 112:5

Discretion will preserve you; understanding will keep you...
Proverbs 2:11

Discretion is not developed simply from intelligence and good man-
ners. Godly discretion comes from God, not from human ingenuity. You
cannot, in and of yourself, determine to be discreet in everything you
do. Your human wisdom will not sustain you through an entire week of
life without making an error in judgment. But, as you are walking in
the Spirit and are filled with the fruit of His Spirit, then you are able by
God's Spirit to communicate from a sincere heart the right thing at the
right time.

Guiding Thoughts

First, *discretion is the ability to know the right action for each oc-
casion.* But, how would you know the right action to take every time?
You won't!

God, however, is not confused about what you ought to be thinking,
saying, doing, or with whom you should spend your time. God is not
confused about how to give you wisdom. If God is the source of wisdom
and discretion, how critical is it for believers to be up to date with God?
It is absolutely critical because you do not know what is going to happen
next! You do not know when you will be caught off guard by a verbal
or physical attack. You do not know when a crisis will come your way,
whether a car accident, a bad health report, or a broken relationship.
Right decisions made in the right way and said in the right timing come
from a daily walk with the Lord.

Second, *godly discretion "makes [one] slow to anger, and his glory*
is to overlook a transgression" (Proverbs 19:11). If you are the kind of
person who reacts the moment that someone says something abrasive–
that is not a mark of good judgment. Discretion is the mark of a gracious

and gentle Spirit. It keeps our minds and our focus on sound judgement. Discretion is the mark of Christian maturity. Some people have no discretion. Feelings, instead of godly discretion, rule their hearts. They do not know how to defer–they react first. They react because they are not walking in the Spirit–they are walking in the flesh! But if you are walking in the Spirit, what comes out of your life or what comes out of your mouth will proceed from a right Spirit. This overflow from your life is the Spirit of Christ living within you.

While attending a conference for pastors and their wives, a pastor's wife revealed that others did not understand her situation. She revealed that she was very angry and unforgiving toward many people in a previous church where her husband had been the pastor. She had no thought that others deal with situations like she was experiencing. After giving her advice, she stated to me, "Are you telling me, that if what happened to me had happened to you, that you wouldn't have responded the same way I did?" My response was, "No, I'm not telling you that. I'm telling you the way in which I would have responded would have been determined by my Spirit at the time."

Whether in the workplace, at home, or school, the way in which you respond to the people around you is not determined by anything but your Spirit. If you are walking in the flesh, that's how you will respond. If you are walking in the Spirit, that's how you will respond. Proverb 19:11 is not an instruction to pass over quickly. It simply states that there are some things you need to be slow to be angry about and that it will be a glory to overlook a transgression.

Do you have any people around you who irritate you? It may not be a major offense from them that irritates you. Sometimes simply being in the same room with "those people" irritates you! At other times, simply hearing their name pronounced irritates you. That is not walking in the Spirit, that is reacting to the flesh! Godly discretion is part of the evidence that you have been walking in the Spirit and you are full of the love of God and the joy of God and the peace of God and the gentleness and patience of God.

Our human strength cannot produce the Christian life. The Spirit-filled life is something totally outside of ourselves–in fact, it is out of this world. It is the Spirit of Christ! It is not our human flesh! His Spirit in you is what allows you to walk in the way you ought to walk. The Spirit of Christ is even available to you when things are not going well.

Jesus clearly presented this truth in Matthew 5:38-48. He called for us to offer another cheek to personal enemies. Many say, "I'll turn one cheek and then the other–after that I'm going to hit them!" But, that is *not* Christ's intention. Jesus said not to resist evil when it is a personal offense against you. He said to do good to your personal enemies, pray for your enemies, and to love your enemies. Godly discretion protects you from acting in the flesh toward the people who have offended you. Spiritual people glory in forgiving and they are glorious in forgiveness. They are the true sons of God. Godly discretion gives us the ability to choose our words, our attitudes, and actions, more carefully and to model goodness and righteousness for any given situation. With this character we will be able to recognize and avoid wrong attitudes that might create objectionable words and actions which would appear condescending to others and could bring serious consequences to relationships. The love of God is kind. Godly discretion is slow to anger. A personality that is quick to be angry at people does not receive that spirit from God. Godly discretion makes you slow to anger. It puts in reserve your human spirit so that you do as Paul said in Galatians 5:16, "walk in the Spirit and you will not fulfill the desires of the flesh."

Attempting to not walk in the flesh so you will be a better Christian is not the goal. Walk in the Spirit and you will not fulfill the desires of the flesh. Spend time with God to understand what He is developing in you through His Spirit. Character development is absolutely critical to knowing God's ways.

The way you live this week will determine the foundation for how you live the following week. The way you live this week is the beginning of a new walk with the Lord. How will you face the next crisis? That will be determined by your spirit at the time of the event. Godly discretion is a benefit of a personal relationship with the Lord Jesus Christ. As you walk with Him, great victories are in your future.

God's Victory in You

ιc times of revival flowed through Boston in 1909. Today, it is ι. ι as the Boston Awakening. Dr. J. Wilbur Chapman, pastor and evangelist, was a prominent personality in the era of that revival. You might know a gospel song he authored:

One Day

One day when heaven was filled with His praises,
One day when sin was as black as could be,
Jesus came forth to be born of a virgin,
Dwelt amongst men, my example is He.
Chorus:
Living, He loved me; dying, He saved me;
Buried, He carried my sins far away,
Rising, He justified freely forever;
One day He's coming, Oh, glorious day!

Chapman believed in a simultaneous work of God. He encouraged all the churches to have meetings at the same time and preach on the subject of holiness while praying God would bring a great revival.

An incredible inspirational writing was printed and distributed throughout Boston during this time of revival. While we do not know who wrote it, the city of Boston was saturated with this powerful message that instructed believers concerning a victorious life.

Imagine what would happen in our day if we used the godly discretion that is represented here:

Victory

When you are forgotten, or neglected, or purposely set at naught, and you smile inwardly, glorying in the insult or the oversight—That is Victory!
(John 13:26-30; 2 Timothy 4:16-18)

When your good is evil spoken of, when your wishes are crossed, your taste offended, your advice disregarded, your opinions ridiculed, and you take it all in patient and loving silence—That is Victory!
(John 8:48-50; 2 Timothy 4:16-18; 2 Peter 2:20-21)

When you can bear with any discord, any irregularity and un-punctuality, any annoyance–and are content with any food, any raiment, any climate, any society, any solitude, any interruption– That is Victory!

(Philippians 4:11-13; Hebrews 11:3-11; Acts 27:21-25; 2 Corinthians 4:8-10)

When you never care to refer to yourself in conversation or to record your own good works, or to itch after commendation, when you can truly "love to be unknown"–That is Victory!
(Galatians 2:20; 6:14)[1]

Are you slow to anger? Are you quick to respond in defiance? Is there any godly discretion in your life? Are you looking for recognition? Are you looking for approval, or are you satisfied to walk in service to your Lord and Savior Jesus Christ and be approved by Him?

---

1. Printed and handed out during Boston's Awakening of 1909 under guidance of Dr. J. Wilbur Chapman: original–source unknown. Given to me by Devin Bell during doctoral residency at Gordon-Conwell Theological Seminary.

Chapter Four

Reveal Or Conceal Your Reactions?

Do you have trouble reacting before you think? All of us have struggles with the flesh, yet we do not have the same intensity of struggles with the same issues. We must learn how to live and walk in a way that keeps us from fulfilling the desires of the flesh.

The psalmist helps us see what kind of person can walk in the Spirit. The writer puts it this way,

> Lord, who may abide in Your tabernacle? Who may dwell in Your holy hill? He who walks uprightly, and works righteousness, and speaks the truth in his heart."

Psalm 15:1-2

The integrity of the truth of God living in your heart should bring clarity to life. Speaking the *truth in your heart* is not the same as telling everyone everything you know! Just because you know something in your mind, does not mean it is intended for a public announcement. Some think that they are not honest if they do not tell everything they know. Personally, I am glad that everyone does not know what everyone else is thinking!

Can you imagine walking around all week with a video screen attached to your brain so that everyone could see what you are thinking? I don't think too many people would leave their home! If everyone saw everything God sees, there would be a much higher crime rate!

As you walk in the Spirit with honesty, integrity of heart, uprightness, and truthfulness–what comes out of your mouth will proceed from a heart that is walking in the Spirit. When that happens you will be glad to share what you are thinking and others will be glad to hear the truth you are contemplating.

The world views honesty and truthfulness completely different than God describes in the Scripture. How many times have you heard people say these things?

1. "Honest to God!" In other words, we are attempting to convince others that what we are about to say is truthful.
2. "Cross my heart." "Really, you need to believe me."
3. In our wedding vows people say, "I do." In our day we ask, "For how long?"
4. "I swear on my mother's grave."
5. "I will pray for you." Many times we forget what their request was and we never follow through.

Here are some other irrational thoughts on the subject of honesty and truth from the world's perspective.

1. "Always tell the truth even if you have to make it up."
2. Samuel Goldwin said, "I don't want yes men around me. I want everyone to tell the truth even if it costs him his job."
3. The modern day philosopher, Groucho Marx said, "The secret of life is honesty and fair dealing. If you can fake that, you've got it made."
4. Will Rogers said, "If you find yourself in a hole, stop digging." "The quickest way to double your money is to fold it and put it back in your pocket." He also said, "Lettin' the cat outta the bag is a whole lot easier than puttin' it back."

There is not much integrity of heart concerning truth and honesty. We become accustomed to using clichés in our life for the purpose of attempting to convince other people that we truly are honest. When you speak, think, or act, you reveal the condition of your spirit. But do we really need to reveal our spirit all of the time? Is there a time that we need to conceal, instead of reveal?

Christian thinking does not mean that if you are a Christian and you also have the ability to think, then your thinking is Christian. True Christian thinking is centered around the truth of God's Word. The Bible becomes your guide to thinking, not what you want the Bible to say! Having your mind centered on the truth of God's Word results in a mind that is penetrated by truth. A person who walks uprightly in righteousness, integrity of heart, and truth, lives according to God's Word, not as stated by the best human thinking. The truth based on the biblical standard can be shared with impact no matter where you go, whom you are talking to, or what culture is present.

Walking in the Spirit enables you to live an honest and truthful life that brings encouragement to others. Yet, people sometimes reveal their reactions in harmful ways. If they think bad thoughts about you, they think they should reveal their thinking. Many have wrong feelings in their heart toward their spouse, kids, parents, pastor, teachers, or a person at work. It is not always acceptable to share that information. If you are walking in the Spirit, God will put a *check* in your Spirit giving you the ability to withhold some things that are not ready to be shared. Timing is more important than time. Just because you know something does not mean that everybody else has to know. There are some things that are truth but they are better kept between you and God. When you know a truth, even though it may be a negative about a person, begin to pray for that person and ask God to help them.

Often believers are crushed by the words of other believers. Insensitive believers feel it is okay to tell others what they are thinking. But there is a time to conceal your reactions. Concealing requires godly discretion and does not mean you must "stuff your reactions." Attempting to control yourself by simply trying to manage your feelings is an act of the will but not necessarily walking in the Spirit. Instead, consider sharing the thought with God. Revealing your heart to God instead of the other person can be a very positive action. The old hymn states, "take it to The Lord in prayer." If you are thinking negatively toward someone, perhaps you should reveal your heart to God and ask Him to manage, control, and fill you so that what comes out of your life will be things that are:

...true, whatever things are noble, whatever things are just, whatever things are pure, whatever things are lovely, whatever things are of good report, if there is any virtue and if there is anything praiseworthy–meditate on these things.

Philippians 4:8

Walk Uprightly?

"He who walks uprightly..."

Psalm 15:2

The Psalmist is not teaching us how to have good posture. He is demonstrating through inspirational writing how we must have integrity of heart. God does not want us to walk in a crooked, sinful way. He wants us to walk in righteousness with Him so that what comes out of our life is a reflection of a relationship with God. Do not slither around like a snake, walk uprightly with the Heavenly Father.

Before you can work righteousness you must be righteous. Attempting to walk in the Spirit by doing right things, even though the heart is sinful, results in self-righteousness. If a person is thinking evil, stirred up with anger, bitterness, resentment, or an unforgiving spirit, righteousness will not be the resulting product. You cannot walk uprightly and do works of righteousness when your spirit is complaining. It is absolutely impossible to walk in the Spirit and be a complaining personality. He who walks uprightly will be the one who works righteousness and speaks the truth in his heart.

The word *heart* refers to one's innermost being. It is the center of who you are as a person. You have to learn to speak the truth in your heart before you can speak the truth to others. All the resources of the Spirit of God live within a believer at all times. The Holy Spirit's presence will never depart from a person whose been born again. Yet, even though the Spirit of God has taken up residence in the life of a believer, there are times when a believer does not sense His presence.

In those times when we stray from God, there comes a conflict within that makes us uneasy. The reason for the troubled discord is that the Spirit of Christ living in us is in conflict with our wrong thinking and wrong living. The integrity of God Himself brings that conflict. When you live a sinful life, you are dishonest with the Spirit that lives within. Put another way, if Christ lives in you but you live as though He does not, you are a dishonest person.

Honesty is the best policy is a well known cliché. That is a half truth. Being honest because that is the best policy is not as powerful as being honest because you are an honest person! If your outward life matches up with the Spirit of Christ living in you, then you are a person of integrity and honesty. Paul said,

> *I have been crucified with Christ; it is no longer I who live, but Christ lives in me; and the life which I now live in the flesh I live by faith in the Son of God, who loved me and gave Himself for me.*

Galatians 2:20

If what is coming out of your life as a believer doesn't match up with the fruit of the Spirit of Christ living within you, then you are being dishonest to who you are in Christ. We must learn to walk in the Spirit so we will not fulfill the desires of the flesh. What comes out of our life should be an accurate reflection of Christ living in us. What if every time a crisis came your way, your response was God's response? If you are *walking uprightly* and living in righteousness, then what comes out of your life reveals the truth of your walk with Christ. Living up to who you are in Jesus Christ is the goal.

Why is it important to learn to walk with integrity of heart? When Jesus came into your life He did not save you so that you could live a sinful life. That was not His purpose. His purpose was to save you from your sins. Christ wants you to live in such a way that no matter what happens around you, whether people are attacking you (and they will), whether people are offending you (and they will), no matter what they are saying about you or doing to you–living by the power of His Spirit never ceases. Do you believe that can happen? Intellectually we believe that we can live by the power of His Spirit, but the question is are we practically living that way? Are we being honest and truthful in our relationship with Christ?

When you are not honest, you respond to the Holy Spirit's conviction of your sinful acts. But, if you are walking in the flesh, with no integrity of heart, it is difficult to admit when you are wrong. This condition makes it difficult to be honest to God and results in the loss of the benefit of repentance. To repent of your sin is the most wonderful thing in the world that can happen–because God can free you of your sin. But, if you conceal your reactions and act as though God does not really know what you are thinking, you will miss out on the great benefit of walking in the Spirit.

I remember a time in my life when God was convicting me of my sin. I was an angry, bitter, resentful, unforgiving young man. I couldn't be honest with God about my sin. I was thinking that if that guy hadn't treated me this way, I wouldn't be acting this way. But while I was thinking that, I still had sin in my heart. I was not honest with God. I tried to convince God that it was okay for me to remain in my condition.

Does God know what you are thinking right now? Does God know what you are planning right now? Yes! What's the use of trying to fool God? If there is dishonesty in your heart, get rid of it through repentance. For years I resisted admitting the truth about my life. I was trying to conceal my reactions. I didn't want anyone around me to know my condition, and I certainly didn't want God to know that I was an angry man.

God speaks in a still small voice, that is not very still and not very small. When God speaks, His voice goes with you no matter where you go. It is true, you can run, but you can't hide! God broke through my false thinking and helped me to see that my problem was not that I was *angry at a man,* my problem was that *I was an angry man*! There is a huge difference between those two positions. For the first time in years I could say, "Oh God you are right and I am wrong." My heart began to line up with the character of Christ living in me. I began to see myself for who I really was–a person who had the power of Christ within.

Application

Do you reveal or conceal your reactions? Either the flesh or the Spirit responds when your way is frustrated. Observe yourself when someone cuts you off in traffic. You will either reveal or conceal your actions. Dr. Henry Brandt used to say, "Locate yourself." So, locate yourself when someone says something to you that you do not want to hear. What happens next in your life will reveal what is in your heart.

Learn to walk uprightly and stay up to date with God. Consider saying to God something like this, "Look at my heart I'm sinful, I'm angry, I'm unloving, I'm a complainer, I'm yelling, I'm fighting, or I'm arguing. Lord I don't have any peace in my life. I've lost the joy of my salvation. I don't love like I used to love. I don't walk like I used to walk." Observe yourself and turn quickly to God. Tell Him you do not want to live by the flesh anymore–you want to walk in His Spirit. Tell Him you want to walk uprightly, and do works of righteousness. Sincerely say this to God, "I want to speak and live up to the truth in my heart. When I see who I am in Christ, I want to line up with the character of Christ who lives in me."

Does you want to live that way? I do. This is a lifelong learning task. This lifestyle is one that builds a relationship with Christ moment-by-moment and day-by-day. There are no mature Christians. There are maturing Christians but no mature Christians. Just when you think that you have achieved everything in your Christian walk, that's when you tend to fall. Be careful when you are on the mountaintop in your spiritual experience with God. The greatest danger that we have is not when we are in the valley. When we are in the valley and fall down we cannot fall very far. But when we are on the mountaintop and fall, it is a long way down. Our greatest danger of walking in the Spirit or, staying on the mountaintop, is to decide that we are going to take a detour of our own. It can be tragic but it does not have to be.

You don't have to walk in the flesh, but you can if you want. To tell God the truth is real prayer. Get real with God by saying something like, "Oh God I see what You see and I don't want to live this way anymore. I want You to change and fill me. I want You to control me by Your Spirit."

You will either reveal or conceal your actions. Observe yourself this week and ask God to convict you the moment you commit sin. Next, observe how you respond to that conviction. God may have revealed something in your heart as you read this chapter. You know it isn't right. Maybe you have been judgmental, dishonest, or disobedient to parents.

Maybe you have been rebellious against the authority God placed over you, or you have been complaining about your job, your spouse, your kids, or your work. Maybe you have been arrogant and proud and said "Look what I've accomplished!" Maybe you have committed adultery physically or have looked lustfully at someone.

Whatever it is, when God convicts you, He does not convict you of that sin to condemn you. He does it to redeem you! Be honest to God in your prayer and say, "God this is what I'm like. You're right and I'm wrong. I want to repent. I want You to cleanse me. I want You to fill me and teach me this week how to walk in the Spirit closer than I did the week before. But Lord, don't stop there. Teach me every day, moment-by-moment how to walk in the Spirit so I won't fulfill the desire of the flesh. Teach me when to reveal and when to conceal."

Chapter Five

The Strength of Humility

Therefore, as the elect of God, holy and beloved, put on tender mercies, kindness, humility, meekness, longsuffering...
Colossians 3:12

Once there was a man who was considered the most humble person in his church. People recognized him as a man after God's own heart. The members wanted to do something to recognize him for his wonderful spirit. They gave him a pin to wear that recognized his humility. He wore it to church the next week and they took it away from him for being proud! It doesn't take much to move you from humble to proud. You think you achieve humility, and then you become proud of it–and it is gone! I have discovered that no matter how hard I try to be humble, I cannot in my own strength. Humility has nothing to do with me controlling myself, but it is the strength and power of the Holy Spirit to control me.

Modern world philosophy seeks to get ahead in this world by focusing on personal strengths–exalting oneself. People want to be known for something in this world, thinking they will feel better about themselves if only they are recognized. So, they attempt to get ahead in life by exalting themselves. They think, "If I can just push myself in front of everyone else or if I can let them know how good I am at a certain thing, maybe I can get what I'm wanting out of life." The desire to show your strengths, show what you can do, and show what you can achieve, will drive you to see the best of your abilities. Christ had a different view-point. He said to put on humility instead of focusing on self.

The wisdom of the world does not produce godly wisdom or humility. Here are a few examples of worldly wisdom:

1. One man said, "If only I had a little humility I'd be perfect."
2. You might feel humbled if your twin sister forgets your birthday.
3. You might feel humbled if you call the suicide prevention number and they put you on hold.
4. You might feel humbled when your horn goes off accidentally and remains stuck as you follow a group of Hell's Angels on the freeway.

Serving on a church staff has uncovered many humbling events. Bulletins and announcements have a way of bringing pastors and staff back to the reality of fallibility. You feel humbled when the church bulletins have already been distributed and you read this:

1. Remember in prayer the many who are sick of our church and community.
2. For those who have children and don't know it, we have a nursery downstairs.
3. This afternoon there will be meetings in the south and north ends of the church. Children will be baptized at both ends.
4. Weight Watchers will be held at the church. Please use double doors at the side entrance.
5. The senior choir invites anyone who enjoys sinning to join the choir.

While these bulletin bloopers can cause a form of humility, it is quite different to have humility caused by the Spirit of God. Can you remember times in your life when God humbled you? Those moments should be as clear as any other memorable event in your life. God's activity in your life let you know that He was in control and you were not–and it brought strength to your life. Through that humbling experience, God taught you that He can be everything you need Him to be in your life. Recall and review those moments often to help you stay focused on God, rather than self.

Define Humility

Humility is difficult to describe. Many words are required from the English language to adequately portray the meaning of humility. A one word definition simply does not suffice. Does humility simply mean that one is to strive toward being a kind, meek, and caring person? If not, what does it mean for an individual to be humble? How would you know if you are humble? What can a human being do to make themselves humble? Can you take action with your own strength and abilities to create humility? Can we humble ourselves? God stated it this way:

If My people who are called by My name will humble themselves, and pray and seek My face, and turn from their wicked ways, then I will hear from heaven, and will forgive their sin and heal their land.

2 Chronicles 7:14

2 Chronicles 7:14 describes a humble action. It means to bend the knee, to bring down (low) into subjection, or humble (self). This humble action represents a humble spirit in this passage. But, there can be a a humble action without a humble spirit. In Colossians 3:12, the word *humble* is best defined as humility of mind which defines a person's character. Humility, as a character attribute, is the work of the God's Spirit in our life–not the work of our flesh. Attempting to act humble is the opposite of spiritual humility. If one desires to express the attitude of a humble person in order to appear humble, then it is an act.

So, what do you do to become a humble person? How do you put on humility as Paul explained in Colossians 3:12? Think of a person you would describe as an undisputed humble person. When you observe their humility, how would you describe it? It certainly does not look like arrogance. Only God can give true spiritual humility. It comes from a daily relationship with Christ. Their humility does not think little of themselves, but neither do they talk about themselves or their achievements. Biblical humility does not put oneself down in order to achieve humility.

False humility is often seen as attitudes of a person who is constantly putting self down by speaking of their inadequacies. Listen closely to those people who think lowly of themselves and notice their conversation. They tend to talk about themselves and how they are not worth anything. They say things like, "I'll never attain anything. No one thinks I am valuable. I'll never be recognized for anything." The focus of their conversation is *I*.

Though humility is difficult to describe, you will know it when you see it. The person you respect and admire will live out humility. Follow them as they follow Christ!

Describe Humility

Some people are of the opinion that humble Christians are people who sit in the background and are unmoved and unwilling to fight against wrong or fight for truth. But that is not true. In 2 Timothy 2:25 the Apostle Paul wrote to a young minister named Timothy instructing him on how to correct someone. He said, "…in humility correcting those who are in opposition, if God perhaps will grant them repentance, so that they may know the truth." A humble believer will not say, "I see a couple in our church and I know that they are struggling in their marriage and I know they are considering divorce but I don't want to go talk to them because I'm afraid if I do, it will harm our friendship." Humility does not ask what will it cost you if you help someone. Humility asks, "What will it cost that person if I don't go help them."

Think about a person in your life who you deeply respect as a Christian. Maybe that person is a Christian leader or maybe a pastor. Maybe it's Billy Graham. Maybe it's your mom or dad. How would you imitate who they are in Christ? You have to follow the God who lives in them. You must surrender and submit everything you know about yourself to everything you know about God and ask, "God, would you, by Your strength and power work humility into my life, and in that humility bring a great work for Your honor and glory?"

A humble Christian does not seek his own. Humility causes a person to esteem others better than himself. A humble person admits to God that they are not sure of how God could use them, but they are willing to obey and do whatever He asks. There is no weakness in humility–because the strength of humility is in the Lord. Humility demonstrated in our life requires God's strength and power.

To say, I want to be a more humble Christian, is to be more like Jesus. We want to be more like Jesus, but do you want to learn the way Jesus did?

> *...though He was a Son, yet He learned obedience by the things which He suffered.*

Hebrews 5:8

Do you like to suffer? Of course not. There are different reasons for suffering. Physical problems, persecution, or personal attacks all bring suffering. But the suffering through an obedience to Christ requires character. Jesus taught through the Sermon on the Mount that we are blessed if we are persecuted for righteousness sake. The focus of a humble person is not on how much one must endure but rather on being a righteous person.

To grow in spiritual righteousness, you must put on tender mercies and humility. How do you do that? A humble person is not so much concerned about themselves, but about the cause of Christ in their families, church, and workplace. Don't focus on self. Replace the thought of self with the teachings of Christ. Humility does not sit in a room and focus on how to deny self. The old monastic system required the seclusion of individuals from the world in order to deny self. Some lived in small cages for years, others took a vow of silence. The goal was to accomplish humility by avoiding any thought of self. But how do you make disciples by avoiding the rest of the world? Replace the thought of self with the thought of putting on tender mercies.

The term *to put on* is like putting on a jacket. The jacket is not the person but covers up part of the person. In Colossians 3:8 , Paul says "But now you yourselves are to put off all these..." Take off the old and put on the new. When you put on a jacket, it does not change who you are physically but it does change your appearance. When you put on the new, you become more like Christ. Put on His tender mercies, kindness, and humility.

The fruit of the Spirit has nothing to do with other people. Being a kind person does not depend on being around people who are kind to you, though it certainly helps! The fruit of Christ's Spirit living in us, not our human ability, gives us a kind spirit. Though we can act more kind today than we did yesterday, it is hard to keep up with that act using mere human strength. Paul is not describing the ability to act kind, he is referring to living our life by the strength of Christ.

It will be evident that you are a kind person when you produce kind fruit. Jesus said that you will know a tree by its fruit (Luke 6:44). If you are an apple tree and all that is falling from your tree is bowling balls, something is wrong! You are causing more harm than good. You will know a person of humility by what they have *put on*. Jesus said in Luke 9:23, "If anyone desires to come after Me, let him deny himself, and take up his cross daily, and follow Me." That means you must get rid of the old and take on the new. This fruit of the Spirit is something Christ does in and through your life, not something that you act into existence.

The real point of humility is to deny self. You do not attempt to stop thinking about self, or think lower of self. To deny self you must exalt Christ. Put off self and exalt, or *put on* Christ. As John said, "He must increase, but I must decrease" (John 3:30). Follow Christ and your focus is on His will, not your own. Attempting to be humble without focusing your conversations on Christ takes you in the wrong direction. Humility comes through putting on the fruit of Christ's Spirit in your life.

If there is little humility in your life, there is very little of Christ being exalted. What a challenging statement! Lack of humility equals focusing on self, not Christ.

Years ago, there was a saying placed over the doors of worship centers. It stated, "Enter to Worship, Depart to Serve!" The overflow of what happens in worship should result in a service attitude through the week. Exalt Christ and humility flows out of your life.

Read the following verses and allow God to speak to your heart about humility. Take a few moments to think on what you read and ask God to apply the truth to your heart.

A man's pride will bring him low, but the humble in spirit will retain honor.

Proverbs 29:23

When pride comes, then comes shame; but with the humble is wisdom.

Proverbs 11:2

...thus says the Lord GOD: "Remove the turban, and take off the crown; nothing shall remain the same. Exalt the humble, and humble the exalted.

Ezekiel 21:26

Humble yourselves in the sight of the Lord, and He will lift you up.
James 4:10

"...And what does the Lord require of you but to do justice, to love kindness, and to walk humbly with your God?"

Micah 6:8

By humility and the fear of the LORD are riches and honor and life.
Proverbs 22:4

Likewise you younger people, submit yourselves to your elders. Yes, all of you be submissive to one another, and be clothed with humility, for "God resists the proud, but gives grace to the humble."

1 Peter 5:5

Humble Christians have attractive testimonies. You wouldn't think of saying, "That person is the most humble, arrogant person I know." Rather, humility is demonstrated by the wisdom and servant spirit in a person's life. Observing a person who walks in the Spirit of humility encourages you to follow their lead.

Humility Illustrated

A few years ago I was with my wife in Alexandria, Virginia. I was to help in leading a conference on the subject of revival and spiritual awakening. Dr. Henry Blackaby was to be the keynote speaker. My assignment was to speak in only one of the keynote times on Saturday morning and also lead several small group seminars.

On Friday evening we were expecting the largest crowd–about 2,500 people–to attend. Many people had life changing experiences as a result of studying one of Dr. Blackaby's noted works, *Experiencing God: Knowing and Doing the Will of God.* Consequently, people in the area were excited about hearing Dr. Blackaby.

On Friday morning Dr. Blackaby received a phone call. He was told of an urgent and critical meeting. He decided he must leave and attend the meeting. So, Dr. Blackaby was to fly back to Atlanta. He said, "Kerry, I want you to speak tonight."

I said, "Dr. Blackaby, these people came to hear you; they did not come to hear me. They do not even know who I am. They are going to be so disappointed. Can you please stay?"

His reply was, "Kerry, I cannot stay. You need to speak tonight."

Ron Owens, Dr. Blackaby's other associate, was leading the music at the conference. I expressed to Ron how inadequate I felt to speak to such a large group of people who did not come to hear me speak. Ron reminded me that the people came to hear God speak. Then, Ron comforted me, prayed for me, and asked God to do something that could only be explained by His activity.

That night Ron shared with the people what had happened. He introduced me and then began the service. I felt so inadequate. I had wondered if people would leave when the announcement was made. I thought that this was possibly the most miserable and awkward position I had ever faced. First of all, I was thinking, "I am not competent to speak on Dr. Blackaby's behalf." Secondly, "These people are going to be disappointed he is not here, and the moment I get up to speak they are just going to turn me off."

When I stepped up on the platform to speak, I was amazed at the presence of Christ that empowered me to share. I spoke on the five-step process of repentance.

At the conclusion of the message, people filled to overflowing the front of the altar. There was no room left at the front and people were backed down each of the aisles praying. God proved Himself strong that night. I knew it was not me. In fact if you were to ask the people who were attending, they would tell you that they knew it was not me!

About three or four weeks went by before my wife and I were back in Atlanta to attend our home church. An elderly woman approached me and said, "Kerry, I have been praying for you."

I replied, "You have?"

She said, "Yes. Several ladies in our church have your schedule and we pray for you everywhere you go. I just wanted to tell you that we were really praying for you several weeks ago for some reason."

I said, "I know why!"

I tried to tell her my story but she continued on.

She said, "And I did not know why I had such a burden to pray for you, but I was praying for you while you were in Alexandria."

I said, "That is the night I had to preach when I did not know I was going to have to preach. Dr. Blackaby had to leave the conference and I had to take his place. Thank you for praying for me."

She said, "Kerry, let me tell you the rest of the story. I have a son who is in his fifties. He has been out of church since he was seventeen years old. I have been praying for him for over thirty years that he would come to know Christ. I received a call from him this past week—he lives in Alexandria, Virginia. He called me and said, 'Mom, I was at a conference in Alexandria. I went because some friends of mine said that I must go and hear Henry Blackaby speak. But I got there and he was not there. This guy named Kerry Skinner spoke. I want you to know, Mom, I gave my life to Christ that night.'"

Two weeks later her son found out that he had terminal cancer.

The power of Christ living in you will empower you to do whatever assignment God gives to you. God takes a humble and weak vessel and uses it for His glory!

Chapter Six

Immediate Obedience

Then He said to them, "Follow Me, and I will make you fishers of men." They immediately left their nets and followed Him.
Matthew 4:19-20

Spiritually you are built to obey–not disobey. When you walk in the Spirit, everything within you desires to follow your Lord. When you hesitate to obey, you miss out on the great adventures of a growing relationship with God. Delayed obedience delays our spiritual growth and weakens the foundation that God wants to build in your life for future obedience and growth.

Christ called out followers in His day and He is still looking for immediate obedience from followers in our day. Followers of Christ are recognized by their practice of immediate obedience. When walking in the Spirit, you do not question when you should follow the Lord and when you should not. Spirit-controlled living focuses on obeying Christ–moment-by-moment.

Hesitation to obey Christ is not obedience at all. Waiting until one *feels* ready to obey the Lord does not demonstrate a *ready to follow* faith. There is a difference between immediately responding to God's invitation, doing whatever He asks, and contemplating, considering, and hesitating. One speaker stated that we have to stop hesitating and take the first step, and the first step is to stop hesitating. That's so true.

Many in the Christian walk attempt to find out how little can be done instead of how much can be accomplished.

Immediate obedience requires one to follow what God commands in His Word. But, there are some things you do not need to pray about! Did I really write that? Yes! Some things God has already asked us to do. We just need to immediately respond and obey. If you ask some people to read the Bible every day–they say, "Well, let me pray about that." You don't have to pray about that–just respond in immediate obedience! Ask that same person to serve in a ministry at church and you probably will hear, "Well, let me pray about it." That is just a stall tactic. As long as you have trouble doing the things you know you ought to do, you will not be walking in the Spirit. Resistance to Christ's commands will weaken your spirit. If you have to stop and think which commandment of Christ to obey, you are in trouble already.

Some people want to live the Christian life, but on their own terms. They want to obey only one thing at a time. They believe that once they are proficient in one thing, they can then work on the next task. Imagine a Christian wanting to read his/her Bible everyday but having no desire to spend time in prayer. This person believes to obey one command while ignoring others keeps them in good standing with God. After all, they are obeying God–somewhat. Sorry, but the Christian life does not work that way. Obedience requires the daily practice of continuing in God's Word, praying, sharing your faith, and spending time with other believers. Jesus said, "If you love Me, keep My commandments. And I will pray the Father, and He will give you another Helper, that He may abide with you forever..." (John 14:15-16). Jesus did not say, "Keep some of my commands." As you obey Christ, the Holy Spirit will abide guide you into all truth–not some of the truth.

If you have to stop and ask yourself whether you will obey this commandment or that one, you are choosing to disobey from the very beginning! Oswald Chambers said, "There are some questions God cannot answer until you've been brought by obedience to be able to stand the answer." God will not break through and overpower your will to force you to obey. If you do not obey the last thing He told you to do, you will not make any progress in your Christian growth.

When I was twenty years old, Elaine and I were making preparations to attend college to pursue God's call into the ministry. My dad was a pastor, but I had not wanted to follow his example of being a minister. I didn't dislike what he did I just wanted him to do it instead of me! When God began to capture my attention for the ministry, I was training to be an auto mechanic. All I wanted to do was go to work five days a week and have a great family life. Finally, the Lord broke through to my heart and made it obvious that He was calling me. My answer to Him was– yes Lord, I will follow You. A friend reminded me that a call to serve is also a call to prepare for the ministry. I believed I was ready to follow.

A man in our church was friends with the president of a Southern Baptist college. He introduced me to the president with a recommendation to attend this college. Elaine and I made preparation to move and attend in August of that year. A few months before August, I was making a good salary. But, I quit my job thinking that we would move in June or July to the college campus. I started a side business just to make enough money until we moved. The problem was that I started making a considerable amount of money. My reasoning and greed took over and I began thinking that if I worked another six to nine months, I could save enough money to pay for the first two years of college. So I continued working.

I knew in my heart that God had called me to the ministry and had directed us to begin attending college that August. I decided I knew timing for events better than God. Have you ever done that before? So, I decided not to move for an August start date but rather to wait until January. The day it was too late to register for class in August God took away every avenue of making a living! I lost the ability to make the money I was making. So, I tried everything in the world to make a living. From that time until December the only job I could find was sweeping the floors in an auction barn for $1 an hour *under* minimum wage.

It didn't take me long to say, "God, I think I know what You're saying. You told me to obey You in August. I have delayed and said I'll wait until January and now You're showing me that You really meant what You said!" We struggled and couldn't pay our bills. We couldn't pay our rent. We had a baby, were attempting to attend college, but were we to do this now? During that time God taught me that when He tells you to do something—obey immediately! I learned that God chases those He loves and He catches them! After repenting, I couldn't wait to begin college in January. I asked the Lord to let the time pass quickly so I could begin to follow Him.

We moved in a borrowed pick-up truck and a u-haul trailer. While driving in the snow, the truck engine blew up. We found some people that allowed us to spend the night with them. The next day we transferred our furniture over to another vehicle. The very night we arrived at college, we had no jobs and $200 cash in our pocket. Next, we received the faithfulness of our Lord.

When I repented, God began to put our family back in order. It is incredible what happened next. We wrote letters to the people and companies that we owed. Believe it or not, I wrote a letter to an electric company and said, "God has called me into the ministry and I can't pay the bill right now. I have moved to attend college and will send you the money as quickly as I can if you would agree to this." We did that to all of our creditors and to our landlord. Without one exception everyone replied that those conditions were acceptable! Only God could do that. As we followed in obedience, God restored our lives.

From that experience I learned that partial obedience is disobedience! Delayed obedience is disobedience. If you are looking for a convenient time to follow the Lord, you may never get started.

God is looking for an obedient heart. Though it is difficult to go through crisis moments, as you obey the Lord, He sustains your heart and mind to get you through the challenges. Obeying God in a few things but not in everything is also disobedience. Remember, Christ's disciples, "immediately left their nets and followed Him" (Matthew 4:20). Obedience to Christ does not necessarily make life easier, it gives you the opportunity to walk in the Spirit while facing the issues with a new resource.

New believers are excited about following Christ with all their heart. A few years later, many are not so excited. It is dangerous to "get over" or "take for granted" your initial encounter with Christ. Becoming careless in spending time with Christ keeps your spirit from being refreshed. The result—living by your flesh instead of by Christ's Spirit. You may think you are okay because you still attend church, give offerings, and pray every now and then, but that initial desire to follow Christ has almost vanished.

James and John were called by Jesus and their response was immediate. Even though Christ healed many people, not all would follow Him. Later, when He went to the cross He said to His own disciples, "Will you also go away?" The multitudes were not at the cross. They had followed Christ for what they would receive, not for what they could do in service to Him.

What if God asked you to lead a group of people who would never follow? How would you face that challenge? God assigned the prophet Jeremiah a message to be delivered to God's people. In advance God told Jeremiah that the people would not listen to the message. What about Noah's assignment? Can you imagine sharing your heart for years without seeing even one response? When you follow Christ, there will be people who will no longer pay attention to you. This does not change your objective in leading them. You must continue to love, teach, and win them to Christ. The key is not what their response will be, but rather your willingness to immediately obey Christ.

Are you facing something that God is asking you to do and you don't know how you can? Rely on the strength of Christ to obey. Christ was tempted in the wilderness. But, Jesus' response sent Satan on his way.

> *Then Jesus said to him, "Away with you, Satan! For it is written, 'You shall worship the LORD your God, and Him only you shall serve.'"*

Matthew 4:10

Satan tempts you to follow something other than Christ. The greatest response you can give to Satan during those times is, "Don't you know that I'm built to obey the Lord. I will worship the Lord God, and Him only." As soon as Jesus said that, what happened? The devil left him.

Sometimes the devil stays around because we are not resisting him. To refuse to obey Christ is the same as being glad that Satan is tempting you to do what you are enticed to do. The nature of human nature is to go our own way. To break the cycle you must return to a walk with Christ that desires to worship God only and Him alone!

Not long after Jesus defeated this temptation, Jesus began His public ministry. As He was beginning, Jesus received news that John had been thrown in prison. This was a good opportunity for Jesus to change courses from His public ministry and run to help John. Yet, Jesus did not rush to John's aid. Jesus already had an assignment from God and He obeyed God with that assignment completely. He continued to Galilee.

A crisis may arise in your life that seems so important that you will change your priorities and follow the crisis instead of the Lord. That is the time to refocus, as Jesus did, on serving God and Him alone.

Spiritual leaders can also find it easy to give up on their assignments, if they do not get the results they expected. Yet, spiritually we are built to obey and serve God and Him alone—not serve the results. That perspective will carry you through the crisis of the assignment. Why? Because you are to worship and obey God and no one else. You don't stop obeying because you are facing a crisis or stop serving God because others are turning away. God is looking for those whose relationship with Him is strong enough that He can entrust a particular and sometimes difficult assignment. He is looking for a response that says, "Yes, Lord, I will follow." Continue with the mission that was given to you! When you obey, you will see a defining moment in your walk with Christ.

Faith should carry us through problems and difficult events of life. One of my professors once said, "Take your problems to God, and your faith to your family." Many times we do the opposite and take our problems to everyone in the world instead of consulting God first! While we attempt to make an intellectual decision with human abilities, God's wisdom already has an answer for us. Don't miss out on the activity of God. You will never find it impossible to obey what God instructs you to do.

If you do not obey God, it is simply because you still have enough of an independent mind-set that would cause you to disobey God. Of course there are costs for following God but you must not ignore the cost to you and your family if you disobey God.

Since Christ has put His Spirit in you and you are spiritually built to obey—disobedience makes you miserable. God allows us to be as miserable as we want, but we do not have to be miserable. Obedience to Christ brings peace and joy back to our spirit.

Obedience to Christ doesn't necessarily make life easier, but obedience to Christ makes living in the Spirit easier. The Apostle Paul followed the Lord with all his heart. Did he ever encounter any difficulties in life? Absolutely. He was stoned, threatened, kicked out of town, and thrown in prison. Nobody wants that kind of life. But, when you are obeying the Lord with all your heart, He gives you the tenacity to go through the difficult experiences of life.

The flesh can experience great battles when you choose to follow Christ. When God speaks, the truth brings a battle within you if your focus is on self. Your whole mind, will, and emotions begin to go against everything Christ has put within you and you wonder what you are going to do next? You become confused. Though you know you are a Christian and want to obey the Lord, these events in life seem to be more urgent than to take the time needed to ask God for help. You might reason that when you solve the problem, then you will adjust your life back to God. This is the reverse of walking in the Spirit and will bring a great tragedy. The obedience of the disciples was immediate, not contemplative. Sometimes we think it through without spending time with the Lord. What will that cost you if you do not spend time with the Lord?

Praying about what to do when God has already guided us in what we should do is resisting obedience. Our answer should be, "Lord I'll follow You, I'll do what You say. I'll give what You ask me to give. I'll spend time with You as You've asked me to." To follow Christ demands immediate obedience. It's not always easy to do. It's easy to say, but not always easy for us to do. The Lord does not wait on us to clean up our lives so we can obey Him. He wants to clean us up so we can obey Him. He is looking for us to give our lives in total surrender to Him.

If you don't obey God immediately you will miss out on the richest truths and experiences that God has waiting for you. The result–years of struggle wondering why you are struggling.

Immediate obedience is critical.

Chapter Seven

Do You Have A Long Or A Short Fuse?

A traffic jam will reveal your Spirit. Observe your body's reaction to the traffic and most likely you will be able to tell whether or not you are walking in the Spirit. When your hearts beats fast, your blood pressure rises, your throat tightens, your mouth becomes dry, and the hair stands up on the back of your neck, it is not an indication that you are walking in the Spirit.

But the fruit of the Spirit is...gentleness...
Galatians 5:23

Do you have a long or a short fuse? It is rare that a person remains gentle every hour of every day. When a believer is harsh and disgruntled it is not because the fruit of the Spirit is not available–it is because he/she is walking in the flesh. You can either walk in the Spirit or walk in the flesh, but you cannot do both at the same time.

Have you ever been to Disney World? It is proclaimed as the happiest place on earth! My wife and I were visiting there and observed many families. They were supposed to be happy in this happiest place on earth. While watching those families we discovered that not everyone was happy. Many of them had short fuses. Their wonderful environment did not seem to have a positive effect on their negative spirit.

Obvious problems in the visiting families of the happiest place on earth needed to be addressed. Yet, to address a problem does not mean it is a painless experience. Suppose I have a splinter in my hand and I ask you to remove the splinter. The use of a needle to help extract the splinter would be helpful. A needle is not gentle, but I hope that in the process of using the needle you will be gentle. You cannot ignore a splinter. The pain continually reminds you of its presence. Hopefully you can find someone with a gentle hand to help you. Some things in our personal lives are also not pleasant to deal with, but need help.

Backhanded Gentleness

Have you noticed how people can sound gentle with part of their statement and then slam you with the rest of their statement? Many famous people have made humorous quotes that illustrate this backhanded gentleness. Notice these examples:

- Abraham Lincoln said, of a man he didn't care for, "He can press the most words into the smallest idea of any man I know." He may have said it gentle but the message was not very gentle.
- Winston Churchill remarked, "That man has all the virtues I dislike and none of the vices I admire."
- William Faulkner said, about Ernest Hemingway, "He's never been known to use a word that might send a reader to the dictionary."
- Oscar Wilde stated, "He has no enemies but is intensely disliked by his friends."
- Steven Bishop said this, "I feel so miserable without you it's almost like having you here."
- Groucho Marx said, "You've got the brain of a four-year-old boy and I bet he was glad to get rid of it."

Sometimes our intention is to be gentle, but we say the wrong things. Gentleness reveals a long fuse. Endurance of a difficult situation with a gentle spirit helps calm a situation. A gentle spirit produced by God's Spirit has no harshness, even in the intent of the spoken word or in the atmosphere left in a room.

Gentleness Described

Someone once said, "Only the weak are cruel. Gentleness can only be expected from the strong." There is nothing stronger in the world than gentleness. This spiritual trait, that is available to every believer, is a character quality produced by God's Spirit.

Though gentleness is strong and always available, there remain times when we are in conflict with others. During these times of conflict, words may proceed out of the mouth or bad attitudes from the spirit that do not display gentleness. That is not evidence of the fruit of the Spirit coming out, it is the fruit of the flesh. Is it reasonable to expect the strong posture of gentleness to be expressed to everyone in our life? How is it possible to be gentle to all people?

Gentleness, like humility, is difficult to define in a few words. A number of languages express the word *gentleness* as the negation of harshness. If you want to know whether or not you exhibit gentleness, ask people who know you well. Actions and attitudes describe the spirit of gentleness more than words. When some people come into a room, people are drawn to them–and for others–they scatter. Body language alone can affirm or deny a gentle spirit. Believers who are walking in the Spirit are attracted by the Spirit of Christ, but repelled by the fruit of the flesh.

The Apostle Paul gave instructions in a letter to a young minister named Timothy. Paul's intent was to help Timothy know how to deal with difficult people and situations in the church. God knew that there would be people who had short fuses in the early church as well as the church today–so He provided this help for them and for us.

Paul stated:

> *Remind them of these things, charging them before the Lord not to strive about words to no profit, to the ruin of the hearers. But shun profane and idle babblings, for they will increase to more ungodliness. But avoid foolish and ignorant disputes, knowing that they generate strife.*
> **2 Timothy 2:14, 16, 23**

When you have two people in one room, you may have four or five opinions! We sometimes are in conflict with ourselves. If that is so, we know we will have conflict with others. How long does it take for intelligence to be removed from a conflict of opinions? Arguments begin by striving over words. Two people are in conflict because they cannot make sense out of an issue. The conflict moves from words to emotions. There is no evidence during the debate of spiritual guidance. If others observed the situation, a gentle outflow of the Holy Spirit would not be recognized. Paul wanted Timothy to avoid foolish arguments that would cause him to get out of shape spiritually. Timothy was to become a leader, model, and teacher of what it meant to walk in the Spirit.

Examples must be set for those observing our lives. We must demonstrate to a watching world how a gentle person lives. Paul encourages us through Scripture to follow God as he followed God. Follow the example of your leaders.

In 1994 Elaine and I moved to Atlanta, Georgia to work with Dr. Henry Blackaby. God gave direction to me as I was reading Hebrews 13:7 (NIV) which states, "Remember your leaders, who spoke the word of God to you. Consider the outcome of their way of life and imitate their faith." God had put two key leaders, Henry Brandt, and Henry Blackaby, in my life. This Scripture encouraged me, "as you see them following Me, follow them also." There are many people God has and is using to teach me how to walk in the Spirit. I haven't arrived, but I am in the process. Observing others is a great way to learn how to walk in the Spirit. Spend time with those who, more often than not, walk in the Spirit and you will begin to understand how this *walking* is converted into practical living. Potters house Lady ??

There was a time when I believed walking in the Spirit simply meant to read my Bible everyday even if I didn't want to. But I discovered that wasn't what it meant at all. I thought that if, "I attend church, give my tithes, and go to Bible study, then I must be walking in the Spirit." *There is a qualitative difference in having the Spirit of the living God living in you, and living out a spirit-filled life.* Walking in the Spirit does not demonstrate who you are, but who Christ is in you.

Paul's letter gave accountability to all the readers and listeners. Paul listed the names of two people, Hymenaeus and Philetus, who were caught in foolish arguments. How would you like your name in the Bible for the rest of Christian history as an illustration of an argumentative person? Would your thoughts during the past seven days stand the test? What if God played a video that demonstrated your thought life for all to see? God sees our heart and He knows what we are doing and thinking. How would your actions stand up to publicity? I saw a bulletin from a church that printed the name of every member who **did not** tithe! Not sure many would join that church in our day.

Paul continued in the chapter with this impacting statement:

> *And a servant of the Lord must not quarrel but be gentle to all, able to teach, patient...*

2 Timothy 2:24

Notice, we must not quarrel but be gentle to all. Gentle people have in them a certain soothing quality. People are very cautious when in the presence of a person with a short fuse. Fear that what you say may light their fuse and explode rather quickly. A relationship with this kind of person is awkward. But, even if short-fused people do not change, we must be people who can be of help during explosive times–be gentle to all.

Everyone argues from time to time. But, the Scripture communicates this truth…the servant of the Lord must be known as a person who is not given to argumentation. The servant of the Lord is known as one who consistently has the right Spirit. God's people need a Spirit of gentleness.

If someone at church shares their sin problem with another person at church, and asks for prayer about their condition, most people will be sympathetic and agree to pray for them. However, if that person happens to be someone in your own family, the tendency is to be strong and harsh with them. To *act* gentle with a stranger is easy. This passage does not say, "The servant of the Lord must not quarrel but be gentle to all *except your family.*" We may fool most people, but your family knows many things that others do not. If you want to know if a person is walking in the Spirit, ask a family member or a close friend. Though they can observe the works of our flesh, God ultimately is the witness to our life thoughts and actions.

After counseling thousands of individuals and families, I have discovered we need a good dose of gentleness. Short fuses seem to be how most people respond to difficulties. Gentleness can help us change from having a short fuse to a long fuse. We need a gentle spirit that brings a calming influence to the situation.

Gentleness Observed

Dr. Henry Brandt and I were asked to be consultants for an organization that Chuck Colson began called *Prison Fellowship*. One of the prisons that we consulted was in Houston, Texas.

The leaders asked us to train their counselors and staff in biblical counseling and put together a program of discipleship for the inmates in the program. One of the requirements for entering the program was that a participant could possibly be paroled in eighteen to twenty-four months. After all, if they were going to be released, then releasing a person empowered by Christ instead of empowered by their flesh would be much preferred.

One of the men in the group was there for committing murder. He had never admitted he had committed the crime. While in the program, he went through the study called *The Heart of the Problem* by Brandt and Skinner. During the course of study, he prayed to receive Christ.

He had shot and killed the daughter of Mrs. W. She was a schoolteacher. Her husband had died, she said, of a broken heart because of the death of their daughter. She had lost a son and now she lost her daughter to this violent murder. The middle-aged man who was in prison for murdering Mrs. W's daughter confessed during the study that he indeed had pulled the trigger that killed this young girl. He shared that he was guilty, did not deserve to be released, and wished there was some way in which he could make amends.

For years Mrs. W had a hardened heart toward him. But, as God worked on the criminal, He also worked on her heart.

Here is the background to the story. Mrs. W's daughter went out on a date with a young man. This young man stopped by a crack house to buy drugs. The daughter was completely innocent. She didn't have any idea what was happening. He went in the house to buy drugs and an argument began with the drug dealer. He came running out of the house running toward the car. The drug dealer followed him out the front door and pointed the gun and pulled the trigger. He thought he was shooting above their car, just enough to scare them. But, the bullet went through the side window and into the temple of Mrs. W's daughter's head and she was killed instantly.

Every time this man had been up for parole Mrs. W had been at the parole hearing to keep him from being released. She hated this man with a vengeance. She couldn't forgive him. She was a tense, frustrated, worried, stressed out, angry, unforgiving person. She had lost her gentle spirit. While attending church one Sunday morning, the pastor was preaching and God convicted her of her wrong spirit. That same week, God saved the murderer of her daughter. God convicted her of being a person who was not walking in the Spirit, full of hatred, anger, resentment, bitterness, and unforgiveness. Mrs. W was convinced by God to forgive the man who had killed her daughter. She did forgive! She called the prison and asked to be able to sit across the table from him. State and prison officials had to be involved to make this rare and difficult meeting a reality. Finally, the day came for the two to meet.

Dr. Brandt was there to observe the day. He shared the details with me. It was incredible what happened in the room on that day. Mrs. W was on one side of a table and her daughter's murderer on the other side. All the prison officials were there. She reached across the table and grabbed his hand and put it in hers. She said, "I'm sick of living my life as a bitter, angry, and resentful person. I've repented of that and I've come here today to forgive you for killing my daughter."

Dr. Brandt told me that there were people in that room who knew Christ and those who didn't know Christ. Prison officials, state officials, and members of the family and community wept as they observed something that only God could do. He began to say, "Mrs. W, I'm so sorry for what I did. I've come to know Christ and I'm a different person now." And he was.

Our counselors confirmed his life change. Once an intense loner, but now after he received Christ, he began sharing his faith with the other prisoners. He would open the door to the Rec Room and yell, "I love everyone of you guys and you can't do anything about it."

He continued saying, "I'm so sorry Mrs. W, I'll do anything I can for you. I don't ever deserve to get out of prison but if they ever release me I will do anything I can to restore this. I'll help you, I'll take care of you the rest of your life, I'll take care of your house, and I'll mow your lawn."

She looked at him and said, "There's two things I want you to do for me. One, I don't have any family left and I wonder if I could adopt you as my son." The fruit of the flesh does not do that! She said, "All I want you to do is send me a card on Mother's Day and at Christmas time."

He said, "Mrs. W that's not enough. I would be thrilled, I would be honored." He said, "What else do you want me to do?" She said, "Second, if God ever lets you out of prison I want you to come to my church with me and I want the two of us to stand in front of the congregation and tell the story of what God's forgiving Spirit can do in the life of two people like us."

I wish I could have been at church that morning–because it happened! Mrs. W showed up at his next parole hearing, but not against him–she stood for him! He was released from prison. He is now a volunteer for that prison ministry. He is active in his church and in his community. He stood in church with Mrs. W sharing what God can do in the life of two people when they are walking in the Spirit.

Would people affirm in your life that you have a spirit of gentleness like Mrs. W? Would they say as they observe your life, "Here is a person who is walking with God?" If not, today, you need to repent of not walking in the Spirit. No matter how terrible your past has been, God can clean up a dirty heart in a matter of seconds. He can restore you and teach you how to walk in the Spirit so you will not fulfill the desires of the flesh.

Chapter Eight

Sweet Or Sour: How's Your Temper?

How's your Spirit? Is it sweet or sour? How's your temper? Do you quickly respond to negative people and events with a sour spirit? Do situations like, crying babies, complaining employees, or nagging spouses, try your spirit? You know what I mean, when somebody does the wrong thing and you begin steaming? You're wanting to honk your horn at those people but you can't find it on the steering wheel? You nearly beat that steering wheel to death trying to find the horn. Your spirit flies off the handle quickly. Or how about, going to Walmart or Target. Maybe you are in a hurry and you grab two items. You go up to the check out and get in the line that says 10 items or less. You know that you're not in the right spirit when you start counting the items in the carts that are in front of you. Sure enough there's someone, they have 15! And you're thinking, I wonder if I could have them arrested for this?

Just that little wrong action of those people breaking the law simply drives your temper wild. Proverbs 14:17 says a quick tempered man acts foolishly. That's the way it is. If there's not a kind Spirit coming out of you, the opposite is going to be there—an unkind Spirit. A quick tempered person's flesh riles up quickly and everybody around them knows it.

There's a way to be kind and there's a way not to be kind. Kindness is not like this:

Mark Twain said, "I didn't attend the funeral but I sent a nice letter saying I approved of it." Twain made a statement, but the Spirit behind it was not kind. Many think kindness is simply being levelheaded, in control, and unemotional.

It is not a kind statement to say to a pastor, "I don't care what people say I like your sermons." Or how about this, "I don't think you're a fool but what's my opinion compared to thousands of others?" That is not a kind statement.

Remember the modern philosopher, Rodney Dangerfield. He said, "I went to see my doctor and I said, 'Doctor every morning when I get up and look in the mirror I feel like throwing up. What's wrong with me?' The doctor said, ' I don't know but your eyesight's perfect."

Those are not kind statements. You can make statements to people that are not kind while attempting to say it in an acceptable form. Has God ever expressed his kindness toward you? It is incredible how kind God is toward us. Is there any reason for Him to be kind to you? No, but He is kind and I am grateful that He is kind.

William Wordsworth said, "The little unremembered acts of kindness and love are the best parts of a persons life." Isn't it amazing how a kind word can encourage you? If you are having a terrible day and then unexpectedly a person expresses their love or concern for you, they encourage you. Maybe they thank you for something that you have done; they express how you encouraged them and their family; they say I appreciate you so much; or a child says to a parent—thank you for loving me, and by so doing your attitude becomes more positive. Words of kindness refresh the soul.

Have you ever heard someone say, "I got this temper from my mom, or I got this from my dad?" No, you got it from your sinful nature. Your mom or dad do not cause you to be like you are they reveal what you are. Your marriage does not cause you to be what you are, your marriage reveals your spirit. Other people will say, "We have this bad temper that runs in our family." Well that is true, if you are talking about the family of sin. A bad temper is not an expression of the fruit of the Spirit.

Can you imagine reading Galatians 5:22 like this, "...but the fruit of the Spirit is love, joy, peace, and a bad temper?" No, because it does not fit with the rest of the list. A bad temper is something that comes out of your heart. Jesus said that what comes out of your mouth proceeds from your heart, not your mom or dad's heart. Saying harsh things to people comes from within. Jesus said in Mark 7:23 that your background, your parents, and all this stuff around you doesn't cause this. This comes from within. It reveals who you are.

Kindness Defined

The Scripture states that one flavor of the fruit of the Spirit is kindness. The greek word *chrestotes*, helps us understand the very nature of this kindness. The type of kindness represented is a sympathetic style of kindness, or gentleness. It is a sweetness of temper. This sweetness of temper puts others at ease and it shrinks from giving pain toward people around them. Does your sweetness of temper cause others to be comfortable, shrinking away from pain, putting them at ease? Or, does your temper cause them difficulty?

The fruit of the Spirit has nothing to do with your ability to act kind toward people you do not like. Many Christians have said, "Well, I love them in the Lord but I just don't like them!" That is not walking in the fruit of the Spirit–kindness. Spirit-filled kindness does not come from human abilities. Rather, as you walk in the Spirit you will fulfill the guideline of the Spirit and kindness will be the natural by-product of a relationship with God.

Many have tried acting kind by saying, "Well, it is true that those people at work did me wrong but when I go back to work, I'm going to try and love them." If you haven't discovered this yet, you need to discover that the Christian life is a human impossibility to live! It is something only God can do in and through you. His Spirit living in us responds to parents, teachers, children, spouses, or fellow workers as a Spirit-controlled person. It is not our ability to act right even if we do not feel right. It is the real essence of God's Spirit living through you. It is like a wonderful fragrance that comes from your life in Christ. Kindness brings a wonderful atmosphere into the room.

Have you ever walked into a room when you had an unpleasant and despicable spirit and everyone else seemed to be having fun? You do not fit in with them! You stick out in an obvious and negative way. Everybody can observe the foul atmosphere. The Scripture says in Galatians 5:19 that the works of the flesh are obvious. When you walk in the flesh and are around people who are walking in the Spirit it will be obvious to you–and them!

One Sunday morning I was preparing to attend worship. As I was heading down the hall, a man walked up to me and began his negative discourse. He told me everything he did not like about our staff–including me. He gave me a piece of his mind that he couldn't afford to lose. Now I confess to you, I do not always walk in the Spirit. However, I was thankful that I had just prayed with another person and was prepared for worship. As best I knew I was walking in the Spirit. I put my hand on his shoulder and asked him this question, "Would you say the way in which you just spoke to me would be the work of your flesh or the work of the Spirit?" He got madder! I have this affect on people. He turned around and stomped all the way down the hall and when he got to the door he tried to slam the door. A return on the door prevented him from slamming it like he wanted and–he got madder! What a way to enter worship!

At the end of the service an invitation was given for people to come and pray at the altar. I was standing at the head of the aisle where this man was seated. He stepped out from the pew and started walking toward me. I thought, "Oh no! What's going to happen?" This man was a very prominent and powerful man in the community. God humbled me by what the man did next. He came forward and put his head on my chest and said "Kerry, no one has ever had the nerve to ask me a question like you asked me. I could tell that you weren't annoyed, but I was. I want to tell you that God has worked on me all through this service and I want to ask you to forgive me. If you want me to resign all my positions I'd be glad to because of the way I treated you this morning."

I said, "No, what you just said did not show a lack of character it showed character." God humbled me. You know why? God was showing me, what He could do through me if I would simply walk in His Spirit. God will do phenomenal things in and through your life as you walk with Him. He can use His kindness to speak firmly to others and communicate a word of truth that will cut to the heart of the issue.

Walking in the Spirit is not simply for an individual, it is for building up the body of Christ. When we walk in the Spirit it affects the whole body. As we walk in the Spirit and be who we need to be in Christ, it will have a positive effect on the whole body.

> *Praise the LORD! Oh, give thanks to the LORD, for He is good! For His mercy endures forever.*
>
> **Psalm 106:1**

> *The LORD is good to all, and His tender mercies are over all His works.*
>
> **Psalm 145:9**

The Lord is good. But, the reference here is not to God's moral goodness, but rather to His kindness especially as expressed in His mercy. Are you glad God is kind? Are you glad that He expresses a kind gentle mercy to us?

> *But love your enemies, do good, and lend, hoping for nothing in return; and your reward will be great, and you will be sons of the Most High. For He is kind to the unthankful and evil.*
>
> **Luke 6:35**

If you are not walking in the Spirit you will not be kind to anybody, much less towards unthankful and evil people. When you see injustices your flesh will rile up and say, "God give them what they deserve!" But, when walking in the Spirit there is a different type of kindness that more often than not brings mercy instead of judgement. What an aspect of God! He is kind even to the unthankful and evil people. At work, or when you go to school, home, or even church, you may be in the company of unthankful or evil people.

What will your response be? Your response will be determined by your Spirit. If you are walking in the Spirit, you will have a spiritual response. If you are walking in the flesh you will have a fleshly response. Some will be thinking how they can get even with, ignore, or even make a special effort to let those people know they do not like them. That kind of Spirit will never breed the sort of kindness that God wants to distribute through your life. He wants to share His goodness through you!

Ephesians 4:32 reveals the type of kindness that we need, "And be kind to one another, tenderhearted, forgiving one another, even as God in Christ forgave you." Think for a moment how much God has forgiven you. God's forgiveness represents His kindness. This goodness of God presents mercy to us. Grace is something that we receive though we do not deserve it, but mercy withholds something that we really do deserve. Not many would be willing to say to God, "Please God, give me right now everything I deserve."

The Spirit of kindness that flows from you toward other people is what will flow back toward you. We will always reap what we sow.

You cannot learn the character trait of kindness by reading a book or taking a course at your local college. You cannot buy kindness. You cannot go to a store and buy a package of the fruit of the Spirit. You cannot go to Bible college and study through a course to know how to acquire this fruit of the Spirit apart from walking in the Spirit. This Spirit of kindness is a free gift. It comes in a relationship with Christ. If you spend time with Christ daily, His Spirit will dominate your life.

Walking in the Spirit requires spending time in God's Word, praying, spending time with other believers, and sharing your faith with those God brings across your path. As you develop a relationship with Christ, the fruit of His Spirit will well up within you and overflow from your life to others. Then, what comes out of your mouth and your life will be from the Spirit of God instead of your flesh.

So, how is your temper? If while reading this chapter, God has stirred your heart to change from sour to sweet, today is a good day for you to respond to Him.

Chapter Nine

Reactions to Disagreements and Corrections

What is your reaction when a person says, to you, "I'm going to be very frank with you." It is doubtful that your response is to say, "Let me pull up a chair–I can't wait to hear this!" Most likely, we shout for joy when they leave, yet what they said may have troubled our Spirit. All the joy seems to drain from us after those kinds of conversations. A word of correction or disagreement can seemingly rob us of anything positive that will happen the rest of the day, week, or month!

Generally, if your spirit is negative, your reaction will be defensive. Much like your physical body wants to fight or flee a dangerous situation, your spirit will tend to also either fight or flee. Your flesh riles up ready to receive a blow when someone says, "Let me be frank with you," even though you do not know what they are about to say.

Compliments however, bring a positive response. Your spirit responds cheerfully when someone says something to compliment your appearance, words, actions, or achievements. In fact, if they want to compliment you, it would be best if they would do it in public so that everybody can witness your qualities. Words of correction for you–well, you want that done in private or not at all!

Approaches from people who want to correct us are rarely comfortable. The soft approach is, "Well I've got some things I need to say to you–but first of all–let me tell you that I really love you and you're a great person and there's so many good things in your life but…" And then it comes. Then, there is the direct approach, "I'm not going to sugar coat this, so let me tell you..." Whether you want them to be sugary sweet, or just tell you what is wrong, you still have to deal with your reaction. The truth is that most of us usually resist facing up to our faults and we also tend to reject the person who delivers the correction. When that happens, we have another disagreement.

The Scripture reveals a penetrating truth at this point.

> *...in humility correcting those who are in opposition, if God perhaps will grant them repentance, so that they may know the truth...*
>
> **2 Timothy 2:25**

Walking in the Spirit is extremely critical at this point of disagreements and correction. Relationships reveal whether each person is walking in the Spirit or walking in the flesh. Marriage or friendships do not cause us to be what we are it reveals what we are. The longer the relationship, the more a person should improve on how they receive a correction or deal with a disagreement. Why? Because over the course of time in that relationship, a Christian should have also grown in his/her relationship with Christ. This improvement causes a more consistent lifestyle of walking in the Spirit. A Spirit-filled person will have more consistent positive reactions. If the way you respond to the disagreement or correction is the same way as when you first became a Christian, you may not have walked in the Spirit enough to learn how to respond to those situations.

Jesus said in John 3:20, "For everyone practicing evil hates the light and does not come to the light, lest his deeds should be exposed." We run away from, not toward, our faults. Our tendency is to shrink away from reproof and correction. When we are at fault we don't want anyone to call it to our attention! Seems like a normal reaction, doesn't it? But, if we do not deal with the fault, or sin, then it affects all of our relationships in a negative way. God puts key people in our lives to help bring to light our sin. This helps us to see ourselves from God's perspective. This allows us to make the correction in our life and return to a vibrate relationship to Christ and others.

Who Should Correct

If correction is needed, what kind of person would you prefer to deliver the message? Would you rather it be a humble or arrogant person? Of course we want the humble person, don't we? It is very difficult to respond positively to an arrogant person. A humble person is a much better choice for delivering a corrective message, but correction is still the issue.

Think of a person you deeply respect. Maybe it is a parent, grandparent, teacher, former pastor, current pastor, a Bible study teacher, or maybe it is Billy Graham. Think about their walk with God. You trust they have a deep relationship with Christ. If that person should observe you doing something wrong this week and they approached you and said, "I heard what you said the other day and that wasn't appropriate. You need to make that situation right." How would you respond? Even if it is a person you deeply respect and they corrected you in humility, the truth still hurts. You may not like to hear what they said, but because of the Spirit in which it was shared, you hear it loud and clear. After thinking through what they said you still may not change immediately, but you can't blame it on a person who did not have your best interest at heart. Everyone needs other humble people in their life who will help them see their faults.

A personal safety warning should be issued at this point. Do not go to everyone you know who has done something wrong and correct them! Your life may be in jeopardy at that point! If God brings a person across your path who has opposed themselves, and it is obvious that person is in your circle of influence, obey God and humbly help them.

Christians who have knowingly committed sin and then are corrected in humility will either become mellow or hard hearted when they hear the truth. If you are the one being corrected, you will face the same choice of response. Your response to truth is not determined by the spirit of the person delivering the message. Your reaction to the truth is determined by your spirit. The safest response to needed correction is to change. To delay change may require increased discipline by God to turn your heart back to Him.

Jesus said to the church at Laodicea, "So then, because you are lukewarm, and neither cold nor hot, I will vomit you out of My mouth" (Rev. 3:16). If you are cold, you know you are cold. If you are hot, you know you are hot. But, if you are lukewarm you hardly know you exist. When a lukewarm person is corrected he/she does not see much need for change. An unrepentant believer is not received well by Jesus.

Reproof and correction are helpful but not painless. If you go to the doctor and the exam reveals the need for surgery, it is difficult to hear the news. No one wants to hear, "Surgery is required to correct this problem." Next, you may hear, "This is a routine surgery." Routine for who? While the bad news is not easy to comprehend, at least it is good to hear the problem does have a cure. The scalpel the surgeon uses is still sharp. It cuts and reveals the problem when it is used. Yet, the outcome is improved health.

When you have done the wrong thing, said the wrong thing, acted the wrong way, or responded to people in a way you shouldn't have, it may be painful to correct the issue. It is not always painless in making things right with God–but the end result is good spiritual health.

Good intentions are not the same as good follow through. The human perspective to problems may seem more sensible to ignore a person's faults–this way we do not have to get involved in the situation. It does seem easier to ignore an offense than correct an offense. However, ignoring an offense will result in a negative impact to that person and most likely to their friends and family. Though your responsibility is not to approach everyone you know and tell them their offenses, your responsibility is to walk in the Spirit and be used by God to help others. If God places a burden on your heart to speak to them, you must obey God. The follow through is critical. Good intentions will allow the problem to fester.

If you are wrong, take your medicine and get well. If you think a friend who attempted to correct you was wrong, thank God that you have a friend that loves and cares for you enough to be concerned for you!

Humble Correction

Humility is the opposite of self-centeredness. A humble person does not say, "I saw my friend do something and it was wrong, but I'm afraid if I go and talk to them they will not like me anymore." That is not humility, that is self-centeredness. Possibly a friend is contemplating a break from the church . Humility asks a serious question, "Is God inviting me to go and help?" Self-centeredness says, "Somebody needs to go and talk to them, but not me!" If God brought them to your mind, He is probably inviting you to be a part of the correcting process.

Have you heard this kind of statement, "I would go correct them but I have things in my own life that are wrong, I can't go correct them." If that is the situation, then get rid of your faults and go help them! The solution is not to simply stay as you are, but to follow through, deal with your own heart, and be in a position that God can use you to go and talk with them. The question should not be what will happen to me if I go and talk to these people. The question should be, "What will happen to that person and their family if I don't go and talk to them?" A humble person corrects because they have someone's best interest at heart.

We must face an unpleasant truth. It is not easy but we have to face it. Romans 7:15 states, "For what I am doing, I do not understand. For what I will to do, that I do not practice; but what I hate, that I do." Many times we need to be saved from ourselves. If there is fault in our lives the issue is sin. Ridding yourself of sin requires facing up to this unpleasant truth.

Paul went on to say in Romans 7:24, "O wretched man that I am! Who will deliver me from this body of death?" Have you ever felt that way? Thanks to God, "There is therefore now no condemnation to those who are in Christ Jesus, who do not walk according to the flesh, but according to the Spirit" (Rom. 8:1). We have to first discover our faults and then face the truth about ourselves.

The Phillips translation says,

> *If we refuse to admit that we are sinners, then we live in a world of illusion and truth becomes a stranger to us. But if we freely admit that we have sinned, we find God utterly reliable and straightforward—he forgives our sins and makes us thoroughly*

clean from all that is evil. For if we take up the attitude "we have not sinned", we flatly deny God's diagnosis of our condition and cut ourselves off from what he has to say to us.

1 John 1:8-10

Sin stands in the way. John went on to say,

I write these things to you (may I call you "my children"—for that's how I think of you), to help you to avoid sin. But if a man should sin, remember that our advocate before the Father is Jesus Christ the righteous, the one who made personal atonement for our sins (and for those of the rest of the world as well).

1 John 2:1-2

People want peace but tend to fight the process that leads to peace. We want satisfaction in our life, but not the correction required for satisfaction and peace. If we sin, then sin stands in the way. Sin corrupts relationships between human beings and God. When sin stands in the way, we tend to fight the process that comes to peace. Relationships that provide the advantage of self-discovery are avoided. The very people who have a close relationship to you, who have had your best interest at heart, who have loved you and have prayed for you, who have tried to build relationships with you, may be avoided because of sin. Since our tendency is to fight against such discovery, we miss out on the restoration available from God through one of His humble servants.

The Acting Response

Christians can be excellent actors and actresses, rivaling the experts in Hollywood. Maybe they have been through a correction that they did not enjoy, did not want to hear, and in which they did not respond appropriately. Many of those Christians (actors/actresses) pretend to be happy saying, "I'm going to act happy just to show them I am happy, then they will think I have changed." Isn't that miserable–trying to act happy? Not only is it miserable, it has nothing to do with walking in the Spirit. Acting is all about walking in the flesh. Pretending to be happy and acting polite to everyone may be the result of false thinking. Christians should be joyful, polite, and kind, as a result of walking in the Spirit, not because they are acting good. If you are mad at someone or do not like something they did, you still should treat them properly even if it is an act. But, as soon as you leave their presence, ask God to change your spirit from acting to walking in the Spirit.

Have you ever greeted someone you did not like? You can shake hands and greet someone who you are contemplating where you would bury their body if you could get away with murder! You can pretend as the Psalmist stated, "The words of his mouth were smoother than butter, but war was in his heart; his words were softer than oil, yet they were drawn swords" (Ps. 55:21). "The heart is deceitful above all things, and desperately wicked; who can know it?" (Jer. 17:9). "But your iniquities have separated you from your God; and your sins have hidden His face from you, so that He will not hear" (Is. 59:2). When you have done the wrong thing, or when you are in disagreement with another person, your normal reactions are to hide, be defensive, or strike back.

Come to Terms

The sin that stands in the way of walking in the Spirit will stop your prayers. God said through the profit Isaiah,

> *Behold, the LORD'S hand is not shortened, that it cannot save; nor His ear heavy, that it cannot hear. But your iniquities have separated you from your God; and your sins have hidden His face from you, so that He will not hear.*
>
> **Isaiah 59:1-2**

When you have a disagreement with another believer and refuse to make it right, there will be a major roadblock to the rest of your prayer life. Praying to God that He will provide help for everything in your life may receive this answer, "Your sins have separated you from Me and I will not listen to you."

Stop struggling and come to terms.

There are two simple things needed to help you get back to a right relationship with God and others. These two things are so simple that they are profound.

1. The first step toward peace is to discover yourself.

If you have a disagreement in your family, or between you and someone at church, a former church member, or a family member who lives out of state, and are not attempting to make it right, **first, discover yourself.** Ask God to clean up your heart first and then ask God to give you instruction about what you should do next.

Don't write a list of every person you have a fault with and then say, "I'm going to systematically go and talk to each of these people" No, first, get your heart right with God. When you do, God will guide you to know who to talk to–when, where, and how.

Be careful you do not take up an offense for another person. To do that will simply bring disagreement in your life with another person. Taking up an offense for others will change your spirit. That person may have offended your friend but the first step toward peace is to discover yourself.

2. Square up with the truth you find.

Confession of sin is common, but repentance is rare. Once you know the truth, then be changed by the truth. Colossians 1:14 says, "...in whom we have redemption through His blood, the forgiveness of sins." Romans 6:13 states, "And do not present your members as instruments of unrighteousness to sin..." The moment you have a disagreement with someone who has good intentions to help you, "present yourselves to God as being alive from the dead, and your members as instruments of righteousness to God" (Rom. 6:13). Offer up your mind, your will, and your emotions to wickedness and you will go the wrong way.

Romans 6:22 states, "But now having been set free from sin, and having become slaves of God, you have your fruit to holiness, and the end, everlasting life." Has God brought to mind a person who you are in disagreement with or who needs humble correction from you? Have you shut them off or offered your life to God as an instrument of righteousness to be His vessel of help?

The first step toward peace is to discover yourself and the second is to square up to the truth you find. You are just a repentant prayer away from being back in fellowship with God.

Chapter Ten

Control Yourself!

Christ did not die on the cross so that we could live a miserable life. The death on the cross saved His people from their sins. This allows us to live a full and meaningful life. Salvation provides us the ability to walk by His Spirit instead of having to walk in our fleshly nature.

Do you have trouble controlling yourself? Is it possible to control yourself? How can we control ourselves? I understand wanting to control other people. We all have a desire at some level to control those problem people at work, home, or church. Who would you control if you had that ability?

People have difficulty with self-control for all kinds of things in life. A bag of peanut M&M's, a shopping spree, a gun show, golf, an obsession for physical fitness, or an incredible dinner can dominate your thinking and time. There are all kinds of things in this world that demand our time, efforts, and our love.

When you read Galatians 5:22-23, it is understandable that the fruit of the Spirit is love, not human love–God's love. It is not human joy. It is God's joy. It is peace, not like the world gives; it is God's peace. It is longsuffering–not your ability to withstand an attack in your own strength, but the power of God residing in you to take you through a difficult time. The fruit of the Spirit is kindness, not your ability to act kind to someone you do not like but it is the Spirit of Christ living in you Who produces a kindness that is real and genuine. The fruit of the Spirit is goodness, faithfulness, and gentleness; all of these are the work of the Spirit. Then, there is the phrase–self control. The fruit of the Spirit is self-control.

At first glance, the phrase does not seem to fit here like the other aspects of the fruit of the Spirit. If it is the fruit of Christ's Spirit then why does the passage say *self control*? Does that mean that now it is your responsibility as a believer by your own strength to control yourself? That does not seem to be any different than anyone's ability to be a disciplined person. After all, people who do not believe in God can manage themselves quite well. Is that the kind of self control described in this passage? Unquestionably, this *self control* in the Scriptures is different from human management skills.

The world has all kinds of ideas about controlling self and maybe you do too. Maybe the way that you control yourself is not under the power of Christ's Spirit, but you depend on your own ability to manipulate the circumstances of your life. One writer said, "Those who flee temptation generally leave a forwarding address." That's true. Most people don't want to get away from everything. They want to control themselves to a point, but they still want to keep in touch with their old lifestyle. If you can put distance between you and your weakness, you can avoid the temptation and thereby control yourself. One author said, "Opportunity may knock only once but temptation leans on the doorbell." Since temptation is so persistent, then there are places you should not go and people you should not socialize with when you are tempted to sin. You can avoid people, places, and certain pleasures.

Can you remember a time when you went to a great restaurant and had a wonderful meal? When you finished the main entree, you were stuffed! Maybe you even said to others in your group, "I am so full I couldn't eat another bite." Then, the waiter brings the dessert tray. Many times we say, "I know I shouldn't do this, but I'm going to order dessert anyway." Your self control gives in. You have determined you shouldn't. You know you shouldn't–but when the temptation comes, you make a decision quickly. Will you give in or have self control?

Possibly a person at work, school, or in your family said some demeaning things to you that they should not have said. They offended you. Now you have to face this situation by self control or by giving in to being like them and responding to them as they treated you. It is at that point that you will discover if the fruit of the Spirit's *self control* is present in your life or not.

Will walking in the Spirit work in every situation? Have you ever heard people say to you, "If this happened to you, are you saying you wouldn't react the same way I did?" No, the way in which you respond to those people who did you wrong is determined by your Spirit. It is not determined by the fact that you cannot control yourself. When Christ came to live in you, He placed His Holy Spirit, the Spirit of truth, the Spirit of guidance, the Spirit of wisdom in your life. This Spirit living in you can guide you into every area of life you will encounter. There is nothing that will happen in your life that God did not know about in advance. He placed His Spirit in you so that you can respond differently than how the world responds.

While leading a conference in Seattle, I observed a baptism before a worship service. The pastor brought this man into the baptistry and asked him for his testimony. The man said he had been addicted to cocaine and alcohol for twenty-six years. He continued by stating, "Two weeks ago I gave my life to Christ and I've not been the same since then. I'm so excited about what God's done in my life–He has set me free. He has given me a new Spirit. He has given me a new way to live."

Months later, the pastor shared with me that this man was going back to his support groups and was sharing with them about how Jesus had changed his life. He told them that the same Jesus that set him free, could set them free.

The same Jesus who can set a man free from cocaine and alcohol can give you control to walk in the Spirit instead of your flesh. The same Lord, the same Spirit, who set that man free can give you everything you need in life. God's, "...divine power has given to us all things that pertain to life and godliness..." (2 Pet. 1:3). You do not have to struggle in your strength to find a way to live the Christian life. Jesus came to give us His power instead of us depending on our strength.

Many do not believe God can set a person free who has been addicted on drugs and alcohol. The God I serve has the power that pertains to anything in life and His power can overcome any difficulty in life. He can control you to the point that you have the strength, not of yourself, but the strength of His Spirit living in you.

There was a man in Luke chapter eight who seemed to have impossible problems. This man had been possessed by demons for years. He wore no clothes and lived in the graveyard. Today, he would be classified as mentally ill and insane. Yet, when he saw Jesus,

> ...he cried out, fell down before Him, and with a loud voice said, "What have I to do with You, Jesus, Son of the Most High God? I beg You, do not torment me!"
>
> **Luke 8:28**

Listen to what Jesus did next,

> For He had commanded the unclean spirit to come out of the man. For it had often seized him, and he was kept under guard, bound with chains and shackles; and he broke the bonds and was driven by the demon into the wilderness.
>
> **Luke 8:29**

Not long after Jesus removed the evil spirit, the Scripture states,

> Then they went out to see what had happened, and came to Jesus, and found the man from whom the demons had departed, sitting at the feet of Jesus, clothed and in his right mind. And they were afraid.
>
> **Luke 8:35**

What a powerful movement of God's Spirit on a person! This man was absolutely out of control. He could not contain himself. Chains could not contain him. He had no concept of reality. He was out of control until he met Jesus.

Christ cast the demons out. When this man met Jesus, his whole mind-set was changed. He had a new control over his life. It was not a self under the control of a human being. *It was self under the control of the Spirit.* That is the idea in Galatians 5:23. It is not your ability to control yourself by your human means but it is your self being put under the control of the Holy Spirit.

When you examine these two words, *self* and *control*, there are two key thoughts. One, the word *self* really means to be clean and pure. That is, to make ceremonially clean, or morally to purify yourself. The word *control* means to have a super human capacity, that is, not one that is learned but one that is given. Purity of self comes from all of these other aspects of the fruit of the Spirit–love, joy, peace, longsuffering, kindness, goodness, faithfulness, and gentleness.

A person experiencing self control is purified and under the superhuman control of the Spirit. Self control is Christ living in you! You are crucified to self.

> *I have been crucified with Christ; it is no longer I who live, but Christ lives in me; and the life which I now live in the flesh I live by faith in the Son of God, who loved me and gave Himself for me.*

Galatians 2:20

Tremendous crisis reveals what is in a person's heart. Have you ever observed people who went through difficult events of life and yet they seemed to respond in such a godly way? Observers may have even stated, "I wonder how in the world they responded that way?" They understood what it meant to walk in the Spirit. Their self was under such control of the Spirit that what came out of their life proceeded from the superhuman strength of the Spirit of Christ.

Hindering the Spirit of Christ within you happens by relying on self instead of relying on Christ. It is so easy to get out of shape spiritually. All you have to do is decide–*I can do this on my own.*

Jesus is the Vine and we are simply the branches. The branch does not produce the fruit. Christ produces fruit in and through us. He enables us to be who we need to be in Christ. When you encounter a difficulty avoid saying and believing, "I'm going to have to tough this out, but I can handle it." Handling something on your own will probably make a bigger mess than it was before you started. Discover and remember this truth about Christ living in you–Christ makes no mistakes. But, if you are not in tune with Him, your response to the situation will be led by your own flesh, your own self, your own wisdom, and your own thinking. This will put you in control. Gaining the Spirit's self control is impossible unless you deny self and meet with Christ on a daily basis.

Jesus is your friend. You are valued by God. It cost God His only be-gotten Son to provide you an opportunity to pray and walk in the Spirit. Why in the world would you want to live any other way than to spend time with God's Only Son?

To walk in the Spirit is not only difficult, it is absolutely impossible in your human strength. But to surrender yourself, that is another story. Christ wants to take authority in the area of life that you keep holding on to. If you keep holding on, Christ will let you. Christ will let you be as miserable as you want to be for as long as you want to be, but you don't have to be. The fruit of the Spirit is available to you every moment of every single day. Christ is just waiting for you to relinquish self to His control.

You cannot live out the Christian lifestyle by living it in your own strength. Christ is not interested in you giving Him part of your life and reserving another section for yourself. You will either serve one master or the other.

Controlling your relationships, anger, a complaining spirit, lust, dis-obedience to parents, lying, an unforgiving Spirit, yelling, arguing, bit-terness, pride, selfish ambition, is impossible in your own strength.

Yet, Christ died to save you from your sins. If there are areas of your life in which you seemingly never have the control of Christ's Spirit, you never get victory over it, then humble yourself before God. Pray and seek His face and ask Him to deal with you concerning that area of life. As you encounter life, ask the Lord to help you be sensitive to any moment you step away from walking in His Spirit and begin walking in the flesh. Ask Him to help you recognize the departure and give you the desire to return to Him.

God, please put our spirits under Your control!

Chapter Eleven

Envy Consumes Itself

Do you know any people who are envious, jealous, or covetous? What is the difference between these three? Let's begin with envy. Envy is the fruit of our flesh. It is not the fruit of the Spirit. Envy does not help us know how to build our relationship to Christ. Envy devours us from the inside out. It can destroy the joy of any believer.

The Scripture is clear and concise about envy.

> *A sound heart is life to the body, but envy is rottenness to the bones.*
>
> **Proverbs 14:30**

> *For wrath kills a foolish man, and envy slays a simple one.*
>
> **Job 5:2**

Envy begins on the inside of a person. Many think like this, "The reason I'm envious is that all these people around me have what I want and need and it's not fair. I want to have those things. I don't see why they have it and I don't. Why hasn't God blessed me the way He's blessed other people? Why don't I have the job that they have or the position they have or the authority they have or the abilities they have or the material things that they have?" What problem does this spirit reveal? This kind of envy infiltrates the heart and soul, and brings rottenness from the inside out. It will disturb your thinking.

Socrates said, "Envy is the ulcer of the soul." A Danish proverb states that, "Rust consumes iron and envy consumes itself." Harold

Coffin said that, "Envy is the art of counting the other fellow's blessing instead of your own."

Simple things in life can attract your flesh and throw you off target of walking in the Spirit. If you are not aware of those simple issues of the flesh and how they work you will miss walking in the Spirit. Envy is one of those things that creeps up in your thinking without realizing the destruction it brings. Analyzing everyone's possessions will shake the foundation of your belief system. When your focus moves from thinking about Jesus Christ to obsession with everyone else's blessings, your thoughts are for self, instead of denying self.

Have you ever observed others and began to count *their* blessings instead of your own? Possibly what you saw in them blinded you from what God had blessed in your life! Envy weakens and destroys a spirit of gratitude. Instead of thinking so much of what you have, envy causes you to worry about those people getting things they do not deserve. Your mind is weakened by thoughts of people at work, school, people with whom you fellowship, and even people in your Bible study group. Consuming your thought life, you begin to pout and wonder why they have things you do not have! It is so easy to lose a grateful heart.

It is easy to avoid having a spirit of envy over some things. What are those things? Things that you have no chance of attaining. For example, I am not envious of the way that Tiger Woods plays golf. Why? Because I have no chance of achieving the ability to play golf like Tiger Woods. I don't even think about it. Areas of life that are not possibilities for us to attain do not distract us.

What really distracts us are those things that come through the crack of commonality. Common things are those that we *can* possibly achieve. Family, friends, or peers have things that you could possess or accomplish. These are the distractions for walking in the Spirit. Wondering why you did not get the promotion at work that one of your peers received can bring a sour spirit, if you envy their accomplishment. After all, they work at the same place. Why didn't you get that promotion? Your armor was cracked in the common area of life. You may not be bothered that you are not a candidate for the Governor of your state, but not receiving recognition for service in your church may trouble you deeply. The wealthiest people in the world are not the ones we compare our bank account to, rather it is those close friends and associates who are in our thoughts.

Envy opposes the creative work of God in our lives. It becomes our way of saying, "God, if You won't gift me and use me in the way I want, then away with You and away with Your work." You may be afraid to say that aloud yet, the way in which you live may reveal your thoughts. Envy begins to consume you from the inside out and brings rottenness to your bones. Dissatisfaction with the creative work of God in your life will ruin your spirit and your health.

Dr. Henry Brandt shared with me this illustration that he had written back in the 1950's. He wrote this illustration from the life of an executive at General Motors. This executive titled a speech, *Getting Ahead– Ahead of WHAT?* He said,

> *Of one thing I am firmly convinced that it is possible for you to be so concerned with what you're going to be in the future that you fail to be what you ought to be right now. And since the future is built piece by piece of many nows, what you are now is more important.*

Looking to the future and being envious of someone else's position, stature, or recognition keeps you from focusing on God's activity in the here and now. The character you have right now will determine the foundation for success in the future. Many people are looking to build their future but they are waiting for the future before they build. God is looking at your character today. Your character today will determine what kind of foundation your future builds.

If there is envy in your heart, it is consuming you. Sure other people may have received some recognition that you did not, but your foundation for the future as a believer does not depend on their achievements. Until you tackle that issue and begin building a firm foundation in the here and now–walking in the Spirit–you will have no foundation. Your focus will move back and forth between envy, jealousy, and coveting.

Suppose a child was writing a letter to Santa Claus. Here are three examples that illustrate the differences in jealousy, coveting, and envy.

Jealousy: *Dear Santa, I had this best friend but now he's best friends with another guy I know and I don't like it. Santa, I want my friend back.*

Coveting: *Dear Santa, last year you gave my friend some really neat toys. I wish I had the toys that you gave him.*

Envy: *Dear Santa, please do not give my friend good toys this year because I do not want him to have better toys than I have.*

Envy desires what others possess and also resents the fact that they have it in the first place. Envy really is a child of pride. It makes one feel as though you deserve something because you are better than others. Envy stirs up the soul and can actually make you sick. Joy then escapes the heart of a believer because of these selfish desires. The result is that you cannot truly rejoice when someone else receives a blessing or an achievement.

Envy will also prevent you from being a productive person. Instead of producing good work, a good family, or developing good friends, envy yearns to get something for nothing. Energy is lost in productivity and is spent on keeping others from acquiring good things. Sometimes, envy is so strong that it may not even desire things for self, it just does not want others to get ahead. Envy distorts our minds to make us feel sad about people's successes and satisfied in the presence of other's failures. This kind of envy kills the spirit of a believer, making them unproductive in many areas of life.

Momentary lapses in walking with God makes one susceptible to godless thinking. This lapse of walking in the Spirit releases the old fleshly nature to take control. It does not take long to get out of shape spiritually. Simply stop reading God's Word for a day or two and you will get out of shape. Stop focusing on prayer for a day or two, and your heart will shift quickly.

Throughout the Scripture, envy was an issue in the religious world. In Matthew 27:18, Jesus said, "For He knew that for envy they had delivered Him." The religious leaders were envious of the work of Jesus. The religious leaders did not want Him to have a following of people nor to receive recognition. Their envy destroyed right thinking in them and drove them to the point that they had to get even with Him. So, the sin that drove the leaders to send Jesus to the cross was envy.

Cane and Abel's relationship was destroyed by envy as recorded in Genesis 4. In fact, this incident of envy was so powerful that it resulted in murder. Joseph's brothers envied his position with his family and later with others. It brought great destruction in the family. King Saul, the first king of Israel, was envious toward David and all the people who followed David. Envy literally drove Saul crazy. In the New Testament, the Jews were so envious of the ministry of Paul and Barnabus that they either ran them out of town or locked them up.

In Romans 13:13 the Scripture says "Let us walk properly, as in the day, not in revelry and drunkenness, not in lewdness and lust, not in strife and envy." In 1 Corinthians 3:3 Paul wrote to the church because they were in such division over who they were going to follow. There was such carnality and worldliness in them that Paul said, "...for you are still carnal. For where there are envy, strife, and divisions among you, are you not carnal and behaving like mere men?"

If envy takes root in the heart and soul a person acts as though he/ she has never been born again. In 1 Corinthians 13:4 the Scripture says, "Love suffers long and is kind; love does not envy..."

Why is a person envious of someone else anyway? Because love is not a motivating factor in their life. The only reason a believer allows envy to come in and be rottenness to the bones is because they failed to walk in the Spirit of God. When the love of God is present in the life of a believer–envy is absent. Love does not parade itself, and is not boastful. Love moves the works of the flesh right out of our life. God's love does not envy–and neither will you have envy while walking in God's Spirit.

So the question we have to ask, if envy is present in our heart, is "Who do we hate?" If love does not envy what brings envy on? Hatred. That person has something you want. They have a position and the received recognition you desired.

That is not a Spirit of love–but of envy. James 3:14 says, "But if you have bitter envy and self-seeking in your hearts, do not boast and lie against the truth." Bitter envy will convince you that you are *right*, while you are doing the wrong thing. Don't boast and lie against the truth and don't try to say, "I'm not envious I'm just kidding around here." Why be so serious?

Verse sixteen says, "For where envy and self-seeking exist, confusion and every evil thing are there."

Do any of us need to confess, "God this week I've been facing some issues of envy and I've failed to walk with You. I've been susceptible to the work of the flesh"?

To focus on Christ takes the sting out of envy. Christ wants us to serve Him completely. That means that we are not working for what will "get us ahead," but what will "give Him priority."

If so, you are just a repentant prayer away from being back in fellowship with God.

Chapter Twelve

The Power of Patience

Residing in every believer is the power of the God of patience. If that is so, then as long as you are in right relationship with God, the spirit of patience will control you. The question is not whether or not patience is available, but will you experience the patience that resides in you.

> *Now we exhort you, brethren, warn those who are unruly, comfort the fainthearted, uphold the weak, be patient with all.*
> **1 Thessalonians 5:14**

The focus in this passage is to be patient with *all*–not most. Do you need to learn more patience than you are currently experiencing? Most of us would say *yes* but we do not want to go through the process required to learn patience.

Spiritual attributes described in Scripture, such as peace or patience, are different from how the world views the same attribute. While help may be gained from looking at both views, the Scripture has the supreme perspective. Jesus said in John 14:27, "Peace I leave with you, My peace I give to you; not as the world gives do I give to you." The same is true of the rest of the fruit of the Spirit. Jesus said, in John 14:26, "But the Helper, the Holy Spirit, whom the Father will send in My name, He will teach you all things, and bring to your remembrance all things that I said to you." The fruit of the Spirit of Christ living in a believer is the One who teaches us the difference between what the world says, and what God says.

The world offers help for learning patience but it is simply different from what Christ offers. Here are a few thoughts on patience from a world-view.

1. Chinese proverb: "One moment of patience may ward off great disaster. One moment of impatience may ruin a whole life."
2. "Some people are kind, polite, patient, and sweet spirited until you try to sit in their pews."
3. Margaret Thatcher said, "I am extraordinarily patient provided I get my own way in the end."
4. "Oh Lord, give me patience and give it to me now!"
5. "If you are patient in one moment of anger, you will escape a hundred days of sorrow."

Patience comes in two forms: human and spiritual. If we walk in the Spirit we will have the patience of Christ living in and through us. Patience can also be expressed by the power of your own will and strength. You can decide to be calm in a given situation even though it is difficult to do. You can force yourself to conform to a situation that requires patience even though you are not patient. The human spirit can be quite determined. Human acting ability can be so convincing that discovery of what it means to live by Christ's power can be lost.

But, it is also true that you may act and look like a patient person on the outside and be in utter turmoil on the inside. Some people, cannot hide their impatience even if they tried. You can discern most people's body language and facial expressions to identify whether they are patient or impatient.

Dangerous results happen when using acting abilities in order to appear patient. If you act patient long enough, you will begin to believe that you are a patient person. Instead of relying on God's Spirit of patience, you settle for the lesser quality of acting. Do this long enough and you become blind to your blindness. Training yourself to act patiently may be good, but it is not as great as walking in the Spirit of patience. The Spirit helps you to *be* a patient person, not *act* like a patient person.

Self restraint is good, especially if you are contemplating murder! But the real power of patience is the person of Jesus Christ living in a believer. Living in a born again believer is the most patient person I know–the person of Christ. He places His Spirit in the believer and gives them the ability to be patient in all the appropriate situations.

Examine the business world and the stock market. Patience is needed by a person who lives and works in the business world, particularly in finances. Many things are attributing to making money in the stock market–intelligence, education, good advice, a lot of luck, and patience. Someone once said, "Stock markets are extremely efficient at transferring wealth from the impatient to the patient." That is true. One choice while impatient can take you down the wrong path for a long journey. One patient choice from God's Spirit can give eternal direction.

The Scripture states, "Now may the Lord direct your hearts into the love of God and into the patience of Christ" (2 Thess. 3:5). Was Christ patient with His disciples? Yes. There were times He questioned their faith, but He continued to teach them. Jesus showed unbelievable patience with all of their mistakes. In fact, His patience was out of this world. The patience of Christ equipped the disciples to become who they needed to become. If we were leading the disciples, some of their terrible decisions would have revealed impatience in us. But Jesus, was patient with them. This patience of Christ is the patience of His Spirit that He left behind when He left this earth. Imagine, His power left to live in us–incredible!

All of the patience of Christ is available to believers every single day. The patience of Christ dwells in you and all the attributes of Christ are available to you. Christ has been patient with us just as He was patient with His original band of disciples.

Of all the laws that God set forth for us to obey, how many have we broken? All of them. But God through His Son Jesus was patient enough to keep pursuing us. Though there are times we reason why it is appropriate to give up on a person, Christ does not give up on us. God pursues those He loves. He disciplines His children. He pursues His children. He corrects them. The same patience Christ has toward us is the same Spirit of patience He puts in us to live our daily life.

When do you most need patience? When you are seeking direction that is unclear. You are not sure what to do, what direction to go, or what the right answer may be. If you are guessing and trying to comprehend what is the right thing to do, that is the time for patience. When the timing is not certain, you need patience.

Are there times for impatience? Yes. I know you wanted to hear this! Times for impatience are:

1. When comfort is needed for a hurting person.
2. When there is a person who needs direction and you have the answer.
3. When a person is without Christ and you have an opportunity to lead them to Christ.

But, though you need to move quickly to help them, it may require patience with the person whom you are to help. In the church at Thessalonica, there were three groups who needed attention. "Warn those who are *unruly, comfort the fainthearted, uphold the weak, be patient with all"* (1 Thess. 5:13).

First of all the *unruly.* Do you know any disorderly or unruly people? You could probably make a list right now. These people are out of step like a marching soldier who is out of step with everyone else. They need to be warned of their situation.

Have you ever talked with someone about something and when they responded you knew they were not on the same page as you? In fact, as they talked it was obvious they were not on the same page, chapter, or in the same book! In this passage, disorderly and unruly people were out of step with the Spirit of God. They were out of touch with what God was doing. They could not see nor understand God's activity. Once a man told my dad, "I just don't know if it is God's will for our church to do this..." My dad's response was, "I believe you–you don't know whether or not it is God's will!" These people were known as the fanatics, the meddlers, and the loafers. But what was Paul's instruction? "Now we exhort you brethren, warn those..."

Another group was the *fainthearted.* Paul said to comfort the fainthearted. The fainthearted were the ones who were always worried about something. They worried about departed friends. They worried about relatives. They worried about their own spiritual condition. They were always worried about something. In fact, at times they probably worried about the fact that they were always worried. They had no strength. Paul said, "...comfort the fainthearted."

Another group was the *weak*. The weak were those people in the church who were characterized by a tendency to sin, particularly sins of immorality. They were weak and easily given over to sin. They had no strength in and of themselves. Paul said, "...uphold the weak."

The last phrase Paul used gives us personal responsibility for these people–"...be patient with all." We have a responsibility as we are walking in the Spirit to guide these people. Helping disorderly, fainthearted, weak people is not to give in to their desires. Sometimes it is to correct. Sometimes it is to instruct. Sometimes it is to tell them, "You need to be quiet. You need to quit talking about this." Sometimes it is to give theological guidance that would strengthen them to know how to deal with the weakness in their life. But our response is to, "*warn those who are unruly, comfort the fainthearted, uphold the weak, be patient with all...*" The only person who can do this is a person who is guided by the patience of Christ. Apart from the patience of Christ with these groups of people, you will not have the time of day for them. You will write them off, or maybe even retaliate against their actions.

Two Kinds of Patience

There are two basic kinds of patience, *active* and *inactive* patience. *Inactive* patience simply waits on things to happen. *Inactive* patience thinks, "Well I hope it all works out." It is like a prisoner waiting out time in a jail cell. "I'm not going to try to escape. I'm not going to try to redeem myself. I'm not going to try to talk to an attorney, even though I may have been put in here unjustly, I'm just going to wait it out."

Active patience is like a soldier whose focus is victory. He is systematically working toward victory. This person endures all the difficulties that are required to capture the situation. Whatever it takes to accomplish the task, *active* patience will pursue. This *active* patience gets the job done.

Have you ever heard this statement: "Well I'm just waiting on the Lord." That phrase can be used with either kind of patience. It can be an *inactive* patience, "I'm just going to sit on my front porch and do nothing, slowly. I will wait, hoping something happens." But you see waiting on God is not inactivity. Waiting on God is pursuing the last thing He told you to do and doing it with all your heart and soul until you receive a new direction from Him. In Jesus short ministry on earth, He did not sit around and wonder what to do next. Jesus actively pursued the will of God as the Father let Him know what to do. His waiting on God was not like sitting and waiting out a term in prison. It was rather, "I have marching order. I'm going to be busy about getting these orders completed and I'm not going to go in any new direction until God gives Me a new direction."

> *Therefore we also, since we are surrounded by so great a cloud of witnesses, let us lay aside every weight, and the sin which so easily ensnares us, and let us run with endurance the race that is set before us,*
>
> **Hebrews 12:1**

That is not inactivity. It is actively pursuing the last instruction God gave you.

> *...looking unto Jesus, the author and finisher of our faith, who for the joy that was set before Him endured the cross, despising the shame, and has sat down at the right hand of the throne of God.*
>
> **Hebrews 12:2**

Jesus completed His mission. He fulfilled it completely. He pursued us with the power of patience. It kept Him focused and on task. This focus of Christ would lead Him to the cross and He would not turn back from it. It took patience to go through it. He had to live with twelve men who did not completely understand Him. He had to suffer. He had to go through the pain. *But impatience did not take Him there. Patience took Him there.*

Does the patience of Christ rule your heart?

Chapter Thirteen

Good or Godly Wisdom?

Have you ever made a decision, carried out an action plan based on the decision, and then discovered new information that made you wish you had never made the decision? You thought it was a good decision at the time, but it turned out not to be the best decision. There is a vast difference between having good human thinking and godly wisdom. If you are not walking in the Spirit your thinking will simply be the best human thinking possible at the moment.

The world has all kinds of wisdom and much of it works. The question should not only be does it work, but is it godly wisdom. One man said, "A wise man can see more from the bottom of a well than a fool can from a mountaintop." While that may be true, does Scripture give a deeper insight? Yes. Proverbs gives incredible insight to godly wisdom versus the thinking of a fool. Comparing things of the world to spiritual things reveals what kind of wisdom is being considered.

Children often do not see the wisdom of their parents. Parents tend to see more clearly than children how to make right judgments. Sometimes, parents watch their children make decisions and think, "What were they thinking?" Yet, when parents think back to their youth, they remember that they acted the same way. When children become responsible adults, it seems as though mom and dad are quickly transformed into intelligent people! It is amazing what a different perspective of life does to change your thinking.

Mark Twain once said, "When I was fourteen, my father was so ignorant I could hardly stand to have the old man around, but when I got to be twenty-one I was astonished at how much the old man had learned in seven years."

In 1 Corinthians 2:13, Paul said, "These things we also speak, not in words which man's wisdom teaches but which the Holy Spirit teaches, comparing spiritual things with spiritual." If you make a decision while walking in the flesh, you will simply be comparing your best thinking with spiritual truth. Human thinking and spiritual truth often do not agree.

The truth of Scripture is clear to a Spirit-controlled believer–it makes sense. While the biblical truth is not difficult to understand, practicing the truth can be. Do we observe, practice, and apply what God instructs through His Word? Or, do we know more about the Bible than what we practice?

Often the people of the Old Testament made poor decisions. God provided everything they needed and He was their leader. He also appointed a spiritual leader over the people. They had all of the resources of God and yet many times came to the wrong conclusion. We often walk out of the presence of God in a worship experience and walk right into a situation that requires a major choice. Be careful, you may rely upon your ability to think instead of relying on Godly wisdom–just like His people did in the Old Testament.

Choosing good wisdom instead of godly wisdom is easy to do. Why? Because good does not seem bad. While it is true that good is not bad, it is not necessarily godly either. Good decisions are often influenced by the desire to be approved by other people. The acceptance factor blinds one from considering if the decision is approved by God.

Israel wanted to be recognized as a nation like the other nations. They wanted to be led by a king as the other nations. They had tired of God being their king. They probably would not have openly said to God, "I don't want you to be my leader!" It is doubtful that a modern day believer would say that either. But would your actions demonstrate that attitude as you process decisions? Would you decide, "God you know there are many other families doing these kinds of things and my children are wanting to also, so I want to go that direction"? This kind of thinking disorients you from God being your King, your Lord, your Savior, your Deliverer, and your Decision Maker. Good thinking will certainly give you options to make a decision, but if God is not in the process, you will miss out on godly wisdom. The greatest downfall in the history of Israel happened when they settled for something that was not the best God had to offer.

There was a time when purchasing a new appliance was a reasonably simple decision. Why? The choice was only between a few models. Today, we research for days to find what color, features, size, and how good the warranty is before making a purchase. There are so many choices. This mind-set attempts to analyze every facet of a decision from a human perspective. Yet, when it comes to our spiritual life, we may not spend the time necessary in the study of God's Word and prayer to make a godly decision. Take time to say to God, "I don't know what to do. I need Your insight to show me how to make this decision."

I have made many decisions in my life that were not the best ones, how about you? If you had always made the best decisions, according to your thinking, wouldn't you be wealthy? What captures many in decision making is goodness, not godliness. It is so easy to fall into the trap of making a good decision because you do not want to take the energy and time to make a godly decision.

In 1 Samuel 12:12 the Scripture says, "And when you saw that Nahash king of the Ammonites came against you, you said to me, "No, but a king shall reign over us,' when the LORD your God was your king." God was expressing to Israel, "I'm your king. I've taken care of you. I've never led you in the wrong direction. I've done what you needed at the right time." Yet, Israel wanted a king like the other nations.

Here is the picture. God's people were about to make their greatest mistake ever. God had been their king. Every time God led them into battle they were victorious. God fed them and gave them something to drink. He guided them. But, there came a moment when Samuel was getting old and the people told him in 1 Samuel 8:5, "Look, you are old, and your sons do not walk in your ways. Now make us a king to judge us like all the nations." In other words, they wanted to be like all the other nations because it seemed to be working for them.

Samuel told them that this king would reign over them, take their sons and daughters and make them chariot drivers, farmers, warriors, cooks, and perfumers. They would give up the best of their vineyards, fields, and olive groves. The king would take a tenth of all their productions. Everything they had would be subject to the king. But, the people did not listen, they wanted a king! They thought they were making a good decision. After all, the other nations ran their business this way, why couldn't they become like them?

When God sent His only Son, He sent a Servant–Jesus, not a king. In the New Testament we read about the birth of Jesus and the shepherds watching over their flock by night. That is what a shepherd does. He watches over his flock. A king has his people watch over him while he sleeps. How far is it from a shepherd to a king? It's a long way. David, who was known as the shepherd boy, became a king. He made decisions that he thought were good but turned out to be disastrous. If you don't know the difference between what God's Word teaches about following godly wisdom and what the world teaches, you will settle for less than the best.

We are to strive toward perfection–Christ likeness. How would you know the difference between good and godly? Walking in the Spirit allows you to see from God's perspective. When you walk in the Spirit, God has access to your mind and heart. God can equip you with wisdom way beyond your years, way beyond your experiences, and way beyond your intellectual capabilities.

When a decision has to be made, what will you turn to? Will you turn to what the bank would advise, or what you think your family would suggest? Though you need to consider those things, there is one other person who knows more about you than even you know–Jesus! He knows more about what is going on in your life than you do. He has wisdom beyond anything you could reason. He knows what to do before you ever ask the question.

Since Jesus knows all of this, how critical is it for you to be up to date with Him at that moment of decision? It is absolutely critical. As you walk in His Spirit, you have access to His wisdom.

You cannot do kingdom work with the world's principles and methods and receive spiritual results. Look at the difference between the ways of the world and kingdom ways[1].

The World's Ways	Kingdom Ways
Pride is important	Humility is important
Do it my way	Do it His way (Jesus is Lord)
Be successful	Be obedient
Be better than others	Serve one another
Stand up for your rights	Give away your rights
Strive for excellence	Strive for Christ-Likeness
Save your life	Lose your life
Affirm self	Deny self
Activity is important	Character is important
Live to die	Die to live
Rule and get to the top	A ruler must be chief servant
Things will make you happy	Character brings joy
Walk by sight	Walk by faith

Godly wisdom comes as a Christian walks in the Spirit of God. It is humanly impossible to live the Christian life! It is absolutely possible to live the Christian life when the Spirit of Christ living in us has pre-eminence in our life! Surrender to living the Christian life with God's resources-the fruit of the Spirit.

> *I say then: Walk in the Spirit, and you shall not fulfill the lust of the flesh. For the flesh lusts against the Spirit, and the Spirit against the flesh; and these are contrary to one another, so that you do not do the things that you wish. But if you are led by the Spirit, you are not under the law.*

Galatians 5:16-18

Live your life from a source that is not of this world, but rather, out of this world–the Spirit of Christ.

---

1 Adapted from, Henry T. Blackaby, Henry Brandt, Kerry L. Skinner, *The Power of the Call*, (Nashville: Broadman & Holman Publishers, 1997), p. 15.

endometriosis

Rice Bowl

top with little ginger

Your Body in Balance

Neal Bernard

you are in charge
- I am here to provide info -
but ultimately its up to you.

Let patients have their own values

older people urinary don't have issues

IBS

to much liquor to heart issues + Alzheimer's